begin where you are

begin where you are

Nurturing Relationships with Less-Active Family and Friends

Jacqueline S. Thursby

DESERET
BOOK
SALT LAKE CITY, UTAH

The stories in this text are true. Identities and locations, however, have been changed to protect privacy. All stories have been used with consent from the subjects of the story. I am grateful for the willingness of friends and acquaintances who shared these tender stories in an effort to bring hope and peace to those who pray and wait.

Library of Congress Cataloging-in-Publication Data

Thursby, Jacqueline S., 1940-
  Begin where you are : nurturing relationships with less-active family and friends / Jacqueline S. Thursby.
      p.   cm.
  Includes bibliographical references and index.
  ISBN 1-59038-222-6 (pbk.)
  1. Mormons—Family relationships.   2. Non-church-affiliated people—Family relationships.   3. Interpersonal relations—Religious aspects—Church of Jesus Christ of Latter-day Saints.   I. Title.
  BX8643.F3T48 2004
  248.4'89332—dc22   2003022550

Printed in the United States of America   54459-7168
Malloy Lithographing Incorporated, Ann Arbor, MI

10   9   8   7   6   5   4   3   2   1

To my progenitors and my posterity:
"And he shall turn the heart of the
fathers to the children, and the heart
of the children to their fathers."
—Malachi 4:6

Charity suffereth long, and is kind;

charity envieth not; charity vaunteth

not itself, is not puffed up,

Doth not behave itself unseemly,

seeketh not her own, is not easily

provoked, thinketh no evil;

Rejoiceth not in iniquity, but

rejoiceth in the truth;

Beareth all things, believeth

all things, hopeth all things,

endureth all things. Charity never

faileth. . . . And now abideth faith,

hope, charity, these three; but the

greatest of these is charity.

—1 Corinthians 13: 4–8, 13

contents

acknowledgments

I wish to express my gratitude to the Lord Jesus Christ for his atonement in our behalf. My thanks also to bishops, stake presidents, and their counselors, who, over many years, have given me counsel, priesthood blessings, and constant support as I have sought it. I also wish to express my thanks to the friends and acquaintances who have generously shared their faith and stories with me for this book in the hope that others might be encouraged. Finally, I express eternal gratitude to my husband, Denny, who loves me and demonstrates that in many ways every day.

preface

A Rescue Mission

L ong ago, by the human measurement of time, there were great councils in heaven. We were all there, and I think most of us were excited for the time to come for decision making about our future. Heaven was a spirit world, and we wanted our spirits to be clothed with mortality, with flesh and bones, so that we could live on earth and take the next steps toward our destiny. We would be able to make our own decisions in mortality. There would be laws, and there would be authority, but whether we obeyed the laws and authority was clearly to be our choice. Our teacher, exemplar, and Savior was Jesus, the Christ. He promised to show us the way to live together on earth and the way to prepare to return with honor to the spirit world when our bodies could no longer house our spirits.

It was his Father's plan.

Many did not like the plan. They were afraid that if humans could choose, they would choose wrongly and fail on earth. Those who rejected the Father's plan of agency followed Lucifer. Lucifer's plan was absolute control. He and his followers were permanently cast out of heaven. They will never have bodies of flesh and bone, and it is they who tempt humans to be disobedient. It is they who tempt those who struggle with faith.

Some spirits who voted for the Father's plan were stronger than others. Faith would be a requirement for success in the mortal probation, and many probably believed and were anxious to learn and obey every law. But there were probably varied reactions to the plan among the obedient spirits. Perhaps some had less faith, and they needed concrete facts and visual affirmations of truth; such spirits would need assistance on earth in order to return to their Heavenly Father at the end of their mortality.

I believe that those of us who received the gift of faith (see 1 Corinthians 12:3–12) were given assignments to minister to those on earth who have less faith. Thus, loving—really loving—the less-active or inactive Church members or members of other faiths in our homes, families, and neighborhoods is not simply a noble act of endurance; it is a matter of being obedient and keeping covenants (see Mosiah 18:8–9). It is a matter of commitment, integrity, and eternal worth. There is nothing more important than to lead our loved ones to Christ. We who have spouses, children, extended family, and friends who have not gained testimonies of the truthfulness of the gospel have a sacred responsibility to love them into receiving a witness from the Holy Ghost. We are sent to gently coax the light of Christ in each one of them until it becomes a steady flame of testimony. We must treasure and feed our own gifts of faith. We must be gentle, patient, and forgiving. We must learn to listen and be watchful. This is a responsibility that can be borne with honor and dignity, and it is a matter of eternal destiny.

introduction

Nurturing with Humility and Love

Christ's purpose on earth was "to bring to pass the immortality and eternal life of man" (Moses 1:39). Our purpose on earth is to assist him by teaching the gospel as we can, learning to have charity, and building the kingdom of God through consistent kindness to one another. I have never found it difficult to love my family members and friends whether they choose to be active in a church or not, or whether they are Church members or not. Our loving Father in Heaven gave many of us a genuine respect and benign curiosity about others. What I have found challenging has been patience; that is, informed, intelligent patience. I am idealistic; I want my loved ones to be quickly enlightened by the Holy Ghost and accept the gospel. I want them to try hard to learn and obey God's rules so they will feel the joy and deep, abiding peace possible in mortality. I want them to understand the consequences of their choices, so they will become what the Lord would have them be. I want them to experience the joy and peace of mind I find in knowing, without a doubt, that God lives, that Jesus is the Christ, that the Holy Ghost is the Comforter, and that there is a living prophet on the earth who really speaks for Jesus Christ. I want them to know what I've learned over time and with experience: that the gospel can't be judged by what we see others do, and that a testimony of the truth comes from an individual and personal witness of the Spirit. I know from personal revelation that the Restoration is a reality, and I want everyone I know to catch that vision.

When I was young, my Southern Baptist parents were open to my visiting other churches in our community with friends whenever I wished. In my teens my perception was that there was good in all my friends and their churches. I was curious, and I had been trained to be respectful. I was not looking to change my religion or the religion of others. When I reached my mid-twenties, by this time married and the mother of three children, I found The Church of Jesus Christ of Latter-day Saints. I was one of those three-hour "golden" wonders. My neighbor gave me reading materials about the Church. I read, I prayed, and I knew. My knowledge was not deep, but my impressions were, and I knew the restored gospel was true. I wanted to shout my discovery from the rooftops. I told my husband, my family, my friends, the woman who cut my hair, my former minister, people sitting next to me on buses, and anyone else who would listen. I totally struck out as a missionary. People seemed to like me all right; but as a person who brought others to the gospel to become baptized and active in the Church, I wasn't very effective.

I am a daughter, sister, wife, and mother. Our fourth child was born in 1970, and when all of my children had grown into young adults, I returned to school and became a teacher. For years I have searched the scriptures, Church magazines, and Church booksellers' shelves for information to help me understand gracefully and respectfully why so many people don't seem to "get" the gospel. I have had a need to understand what my appropriate response to their opinions and feelings was to be. In becoming a teacher and then a university professor, my exposure to people and their varied and marvelous cultures expanded along with my understanding of the doctrines and principles of the gospel. My patience grew, and through Christ, I began to feel peace in spite of the choices of others.

In my ongoing search for information about how to help my family and friends understand the gospel, I have continued to pray for these loved ones, and I have often put their names on the temple prayer roll. I have discovered many strategies of love that can be practiced in order to keep warm, growing relationships with family members and friends who are less-active or inactive members of the Church or members of other faiths. Sometimes it requires great patience, but I know that the Lord gives us the strength and patience and inspiration to be a positive presence in the lives of these loved ones.

I have interviewed many people in an effort to understand their experiences and learn about their methods of meeting these kinds of challenges. As I share their knowledge, it is my hope that this work will aid many who struggle with the myriad situations that arise while striving to live and love the gospel when some or many of one's friends and family regard the gospel very differently. It is an important topic, and I know that I am not alone. I am still not highly skilled at helping the Holy Ghost convert people. I am sometimes temporarily disappointed with that; but my resolve is to continue to live the commandments as well as I can. On the other hand, I have close relationships with all of my family, many, many friends, and professional colleagues, both in and out of the Church, and I know that at the right time and the right place they will recognize that the gospel is true. In spite of the blessings of those wonderful relationships, I feel the lives of these loved ones and my own life would be better if they could embrace the gospel sooner. Regardless, they are worth waiting for. It is vital that we not lose hope in their behalf.

In the following chapters, you will find many true stories, examples, and authoritative counsel from Church leaders about how to love and maintain good relationships with family and friends who are less active or who are not members of our faith. I will share examples of how my family and others have negotiated the bridge between differing religious points of view. The situations vary. There are spouses who either choose not to join the Church or who become inactive after being baptized and sealed in the temple. There are converts with loving nonmember families; there are converts with unloving nonmember families. There are children who choose to leave the Church, there are beloved friends and colleagues, and there are others whose lives we touch. The scriptures and the leaders of the Church have given us much counsel. Some of that counsel will be shared as the stories unfold.

A few weeks after I read about the Church, my husband and I became members of The Church of Jesus Christ of Latter-day Saints. With our children, we were sealed for time and all eternity in the Salt Lake Temple a year later. My husband has since chosen to withdraw from his activity in the Church. He is an honest man, and though he tried many times to gain a testimony of the truthfulness of the restored gospel, somehow his efforts failed. He thoughtfully chose to become what is now called less active. After he decided to withdraw from activity, he informed me that he would be taking our children (then eight, six, and four) with him. He and the children began attending the Episcopal church at the invitation of an Episcopal colleague at his place of employment. He told me that if I believed in The Church of Jesus Christ of Latter-day Saints, then I could continue my membership and attendance;

but he asked me not to stand in the way of the children being trained in the Christian principles and traditions of a Protestant belief system.

There are many turns and twists to our story, and over time I have learned that it is not unusual. Sometimes one of a couple does not receive the witness of the Holy Ghost that the Church is true, or one of the couple decides that Church activity is simply not what he or she wants. We know that this is a world of increasing confusion and temptation. Sometimes children decide to become less active and seem to throw away the training good parents have tried so hard to provide. Some turn to other religions; some turn to drugs and liquor and socially unacceptable behaviors; some become lazy, apathetic, or depressed.

Converts usually have extended families that are nonmembers, and the Church is sometimes viewed by them as something that has intruded upon the sanctity and cohesiveness of the family circle. Often the Church has been misrepresented to them or misinterpreted by them. For my husband, Denny, and me, one of the issues was the Word of Wisdom. The children had been taught in Primary that some substances are simply not acceptable. At that time, all four of their non-LDS grandparents drank coffee, and some of them smoked and enjoyed a cocktail now and then. The children informed their grandparents that they were breaking the Word of Wisdom and that they might never see God again if they didn't stop. I counseled the children, but it wasn't enough. None of the grandparents drank to excess; they were occasional social drinkers. They drank weak iced tea in the summertime, and even that became an issue. Denny's mother spoke sternly to him about the children's criticism. My mother also spoke sternly to me and said to stop the children from uttering such nonsense. Our parents were really adamant, and, understandably, Denny, who wasn't particularly comfortable with the religion anyway, decided to diffuse the conflict by taking the children to a different church. Though that split lasted only for a few years, it was enough to calm the parents. Denny eventually withdrew from activity there, but to this day he remains without a testimony of the gospel.

Many new converts to the Church have a network of non-member friends and colleagues who they love and respect. Newcomers are fellowshipped, given responsibility in the ward, and generally enveloped with new friends. New members often make significant changes in their lives over a very short period of time and add new responsibilities. It is a challenge to maintain old friendships and acquaintances in the same way as before. The effort is well worth it, but it is difficult.

My husband's parents and mine did not join the Church in their time on earth. Even so, we had close, loving relationships through the years, and the temple work has been performed for those who are now deceased. Only one is still living, my mother, and she is a deeply committed Southern Baptist. They were deeply devoted parents who could not understand why we became Mormons. But even though they were not interested in changing the religion of their births, they came to accept our religious choices. Because they loved us, they warmly continued to keep us in the family circles.

My husband's withdrawal from Church activity was influenced by these well-meaning parents, but I did not anticipate his decision. I did not realize that he felt hypocritical looking and acting like a Mormon when he was not fully converted to the gospel. When he told me what he had decided to do, I thought my heart would break. I did my best to understand his reasoning because I did not want to ruin our relationship. Though I did not foresee that he would become entirely inactive, I had realized soon after we traveled to the temple that expecting him to live the religion as I thought it should be lived would be more and more uncomfortable for him. He felt that he no longer owned his own time, and, as alluded to earlier, he was unhappy with the way being converts to The Church of Jesus Christ was affecting our relationships with the extended family.

When Denny lost interest in the Protestant church, I began to take the children to the Primary and Sunday School in the local ward, and it wasn't long before they felt comfortable there. Our parents accepted the situation, and the Word of Wisdom conflicts that had been present in our early years of membership were never mentioned again.

Measuring in the Dark

In addition to family relationships, old friendships are precious and worth nurturing to keep alive. Sometimes waiting for the witness of the Holy Ghost to be recognized and acknowledged by these loved ones may seem a little like "measuring in the dark." The phrase "measuring in the dark" has been kicked around by our family for many years.

Just after dusk one winter evening a little more than twenty-five years ago, I called my family to dinner. The children (then thirteen, eleven, nine, and three) came quickly, but there was no sign of my husband. "Where's Dad?" I asked the kids. They didn't know. He was preparing to build a basement bedroom for our oldest son, so I opened the basement door and called down into the darkness to see if he was there. "I'll be right up," he responded.

"What are you doing down there?"

"Measuring in the dark."

"Measuring in the dark?"

7

"Yep, I'm just finishing."

I reflected on that phrase. I think we all do a lot of "measuring in the dark"—that is, we guess choices over a lifetime.

In loving many nonmember relatives, friends, and acquaintances, I often feel that I am measuring in the dark: I don't always fully understand how they feel about Mormons, or Latter-day Saints. Still, it doesn't get in the way of conversation and shared interests. Conversations can range from children to sports to art, antiques, books, movies, news, weather, travel, and other "safe" subjects; sometimes religion and politics come up, but those topics are handled with respectful curiosity and tact.

My husband and others who have made similar decisions create a challenging road for those close to them who believe in the truthfulness of the gospel. When we love those who are uninterested in the gospel message, we are given unique opportunities to grow unto Christ. I have been anxious to learn what works to maintain good relationships, and I am anxious to share what I have managed to learn. The Lord promised, "If any of you lack wisdom, let him ask of God, that giveth to all men liberally, and upbraideth not; and it shall be given him" (James 1:5). Each person who faces mixed commitments in regard to the gospel has individual experiences and handles challenges in his or her own way. Sharing some of those experiences is the essential purpose of this book.

The Lord has shaped and remolded my understanding and point-of-view as a wife, mother, and grandmother in Zion. I have learned how to build a strong, eternal marriage and family through life experiences seen through a clear lens of love. There are many exceptionally strong, happy families in which family members have strongly held but differing beliefs. Members within those family situations continue faithfully to do their part in building the kingdom.

On the other hand, all too often spouses of less-active members stop in their own progress. "Usually individually but sometimes collectively, because of unforeseen circumstances, we may be held up in our journey, as it were, at Winter Quarters. . . . Even after sadness and grief, as President Boyd K. Packer urged, we are to 'pick up our handcarts and head west'" (Neal A. Maxwell, *If Thou Endure It Well*, 13). The stories in this book will offer strength and solace to those who have experienced the heartache of "unforeseen circumstances" and need to know they are not alone in their hope.

I can tell you up front that successful relationships have a lot to do with respecting everyone's agency. There are comfortable ways to have continued healthy relationships with those who interpret life differently than testimony-bearing members of the Church. Remember that all blessings, including social relationships, are predicated by law (see D&C 130:20–21). One of the most basic and integral concepts of God's law is to treat others as we would like to be treated. The challenge is learning how others, who we often do not understand, want to be treated. Patience, kindness, and love never fail. I hope that what I have written will help readers gain more patience and understanding than they have already found. I also hope that it will help all of us to remember that the Lord knows our needs and will help us as we sincerely strive to "love one another."

chapter one

Less-Active Spouses and the Lord's Compassion

It would be delightful if I went home tonight and my husband smilingly announced that he now believed the Church was true and he would soon get a temple recommend. That seems to be the expectation of many people I know concerning him, but they do not know him as I do. I am not expecting that to happen any time soon, although the idealist in me still hopes it might occur. Yet I know that our current situation is the way the Lord is teaching and shaping both of us. That knowledge is a reminder of my need for quiet, prayerful patience. That is sometimes hard to master, but prayerful patience is the key.

Those of us in the Church who have testimonies and are living the gospel without our marriage partners are surely pioneers. Speaking of the trials we face in life, Elder Neal A. Maxwell explained, "despite the hardships there is a valley that lies ahead toward which we must move" (*If Thou Endure It Well*, 13). I have learned that this effort is worth every prayer, every application of our intelligence, energy, patience, and love. Most of us will share both time and eternity with these dear ones who just take a bit longer to embrace the Lord.

In the book *If Thou Endure It Well*, Elder Maxwell answered a question that I have often pondered:

> We may wonder how our joy can be full in eternity if anyone we love is excluded from a fulness of joy? Can Adam and Eve have complete joy without having their unrighteous posterity

with them, including Cain, in the eternal world to come (see D&C 107:53–56)?

On a much more vast scale, can Heavenly Father and Mother have a fulness of joy when a third of their children rebelled early on—along with many more later who will never come finally and fully home?

Mitigating factors to be considered include these: (1) In the justice and mercy of God, everyone will—at one point or another—have had an adequate opportunity to choose their futures according to the acted out "desires of their hearts." (2) Having chosen for ourselves that which we will be allotted in eternity, we will not later complain about God's mercy or justice (see Mosiah 27:31; Alma 12:15). Brigham affirms: "If we fail to obtain the salvation we are seeking for, we shall acknowledge that we have secured to ourselves every reward that is due to us by our acts, and that we have acted in accordance with the independent agency given us, and we shall be judged out of our own mouths whether we are justified or condemned." [*Journal of Discourses*, 7:204.] (3) Each post-resurrection kingdom is a kingdom of glory that is far better than this world we now know. Even "the glory of the telestial" will surpass "all understanding" (D&C 76:89). (4) The family circle, when finally completed in time for the world to come, may yet be larger than we can now imagine; late arrivals, after having paid a severe price and thus being finally qualified, may be more than a few.

We must not, therefore, underestimate the redemptive and reaching effectiveness of our Father's ongoing work in the spirit world (129–30).

Our heavenly parents experience complete joy because they have all-encompassing understanding and mercy. We have much to learn. With love and humility, it is our responsibility to reach out to beloved partners. We have a sacred responsibility to gain the faith, wisdom, and compassion necessary to give them our best—to make a difference in the lives of those whose lives touch ours.

At a BYU Women's Conference, Sandra Rogers quoted the beatitude "Blessed are the pure in heart" (Matthew 5:8) and asserted, "The pure in heart see the spark of divinity in others" ("How Do I Become a True Friend?" in *The Arms of His Love*, 196). Seeing that "spark of divinity" in our spouses will eventually unite couples with the divine influence of the Holy Ghost.

One of the women I interviewed for this book is a convert who married a returned missionary. He had been born to and carefully raised by faithful Latter-day Saints with a pioneer heritage. The couple met at a young adult activity, dated for more than a year, and married in the Logan Temple. In a few years they had two children, a lovely home, and a good income. The husband then concluded he had been incorrectly taught as a child and decided to leave the Church. His argument was that there is good in all churches, and the authority of The Church of Jesus Christ of Latter-day Saints was no more legitimate than priesthood claims of other Christian religions. The couple has remained married and worked out many of their differing views, but disappointment is an everyday reality for this young wife and mother.

Because of the husband's criticism of the Church, their teenage son has also become inactive. This faithful mother is prayerfully waiting for her husband's heart to soften toward the Church, and she extends constant and responsible affection in the meantime. She shared with me some of the nurturing approaches she has used with both her husband and son. She works to maintain close family ties with her husband's family because they are active in the Church and help to provide constant examples for her husband and son. There are missionary farewells and homecomings, showers, weddings, and seasonal celebrations that she and her family attend. She has also remained close to her own extended family, some converts but mostly nonmembers, and has maintained good relationships with all of them.

Sandra Rogers wrote, "The pure in heart have the Spirit of the Lord, which purifies their affections and lifts friendship to the level of charity" (ibid., 196). The following story of patience and love rewarded was shared by a friend whose husband had been a less-active member of the Church for more than fifty years but recently returned to full activity.

> When I met [my husband], we were neither one active in the Church, and neither were our parents. It wasn't a very important thing to us then. We had both been baptized as children, but we had drifted away from it when we were in our teens. We had to work, and we just didn't go to church very often. He was a friend of one of my brothers, and that is how we met. We were married in my grandmother's home in Payson, and then he had to go away with the Navy because he was a mechanic and was needed in the war.
>
> When he came home, we began having our children. After a few years I began taking the children to church. He didn't mind that, and he went with us occasionally but never had an interest in becoming involved. He was always a good provider for the children and me, and when I needed him I could always find him either at work on a car or in our garage taking a car engine apart or putting one together. He always kept busy. I guess I've done a lot of things over the years to show him that I love him . . . cookies and a glass of milk after the children were in bed, putting the paper by his chair, good dinners, and a clean house. . . .
>
> Several years ago, our home teachers asked him to read the Book of Mormon and pray about it to gain a testimony of it. He didn't do that for a long time. I think he was afraid he would have to change his life if he found out it was really true. [Later,

however,] I started noticing that the Book of Mormon was on the table by his chair a lot. One weekend he told me that he thought he ought to get baptized—just like that. I was stunned. We hadn't ever talked about it, but I always knew he had been baptized when he was a child.

That next Sunday he went to church with me, and then he made an appointment with the bishop. I don't know all that was said in that meeting, but he never had to be baptized again, and in just a little more than a year, we were sealed in the temple. He has never talked much about any of this, but he has kept his covenants and accepted callings in the Church since that first talk with the bishop. He is a quiet, private man. About all I can say that I did was love him; I always have. I have always prayed for him too. Though I always hoped this would happen for him, I didn't realize that he really would become an active member of the Church. We are very happy together.

This woman loved her husband and children and served them. She was patient and let him find the gospel in his own time and in his own way. I don't see this couple very often, but when I do, it is always the same: they are together, often holding hands, and they smile.

A former military wife, a neighbor of mine in an Eastern state, shared the following story about her husband's conversion to the Church. She was raised in an active LDS family and was attending college in Arizona when this dashing young man "swept her off her feet." He was not a member of the Church, but after a short, romantic courtship, they were married by the bishop in her parents' ward.

He was in an ROTC program at his college and was required to enter active military service after graduation. Two children arrived early in their marriage, and because her husband was gone so much, this young woman was responsible for both the children and the home, inside and out. When he was home it was for brief periods and there was tension concerning the children. To the children, she was the authority in the home and he was a friendly visitor. When he tried to assert his authority, the children would turn to their mother for comfort. After he had completed his term in the service he was in the reserves, and his job as a sales representative took him out of state for weeks at a time. This pattern continued until the children were in their early teens.

This faithful mother raised the children carefully, teaching them the gospel and seeing to their activity in Church. One night, long after she and the children had gone to bed, the phone rang. It was her husband.

He sounded so tired. I had noticed that he was looking fatigued when he was home, but he said that he felt fine. I wanted him to see a doctor, but he said he really didn't think he needed to. He told me that he had been crying. "Crying," I said, "You?" I had never seen him cry, not even when his dad died. He told me that with the age of the kids, he was just feeling uneasy about being gone so much. He was thinking about going back to school for graduate work, but it would mean working less and maybe drawing money out of our house. He said he couldn't get rid of the idea, and he wanted me to think about it. I told him that if it meant we could just sleep together in the same bed every night, I could support him in anything! He laughed, and to make a long story short, he quit that job, got a part-time position in car sales, and went back to school.

From the beginning of our relationship, he had assured me that he believed in God, he just didn't like church people. His parents had been Protestants and had often dropped him and his sisters off for Sunday School and picked them up afterwards. Through the years he had attended sacrament meeting with the children and me when he was in town. Now he started attending every week. The bishop suggested that our whole family take the missionary lessons together, and he agreed to that, though I did not have the impression that he was planning to be converted! The Holy Ghost touched his heart when our daughter, then thirteen, bore her testimony after a lesson from the missionaries. Soon after that, he was baptized, and later we were sealed together, along with our children, in the Salt Lake Temple.

For years, I really anguished about our relationship. I felt secure in our marriage, and in his faithfulness to me, but he was gone so much, and I was always alone. I wanted to share the gospel with him, but he was never focused enough on it to feel a real need. Yet, I did receive the answer to my prayers almost when I wasn't looking.

More than anything, this wife had wanted to share the gospel with her husband, and yet there never seemed to be a time. She continued to fast and pray as she waited for a change. She carefully raised her two children. As her neighbor, I know that she fought discouragement many times. Though she did not regret marrying her nonmember "knight in shining armor," it was a long, challenging wait.

Frequent loneliness is an arduous state. Elizabeth VanDenBerghe wrote: "While mutual respect, love, and family unity all contribute to a strong marriage, periods of loneliness and discouragement almost inevitably arise for the member whose spouse is less active" ("Marriage and the Less-Active Spouse," Ensign, September 1993, 19). Indeed, many members find that not being able to share their "most treasured possession"—the gospel—is the hardest thing in life (see ibid.).

It is hard, but we know that we will not be asked to suffer more than we, with faith, are able to endure. If we reflect on our responsibilities concerning those who may not have as much faith, our task is easier to understand.

One of my dearest friends of more than thirty-five years is married to a man who remains less active, indifferent, and sometimes even hostile toward her and the Church. Both spouses were raised in active LDS families in small towns in Utah. They met and courted when they were both in school and were married in the temple. He has had a successful and far-reaching government career, including appointments that took the family to Brazil for three years and England for two years. They have three grown children. All of their children and grandchildren are active in the Church.

My friend told me that before she accepted her husband's proposal of marriage, she fasted and prayed for help with the decision. Not feeling a confirmation at once, she delayed giving him an answer, yet she could not let her feelings for him go. She prayed and fasted again and felt, "without a shadow of doubt," as she said, that her decision to marry him was in keeping with the Lord's will for her.

They were married and made the covenants, but even on their honeymoon, he stepped out for beer and poker with the local crowd. She was devastated, but based on the clear confirmation she had felt, she has never wavered in her conviction that he was the person she should marry. She shared with me her feelings concerning living with the man she calls her "beloved apostate":

> How have I have coped with his indifference to the things I've held most sacred all my life? Well, not very well sometimes. On the other hand, I have learned so much from this experience. You know, one of my mother's neighbors warned her to tell me not to marry him. The neighbor said that he was ambitious and really wouldn't be much of a husband. I have to say that hasn't been entirely true. He has always been ambitious, but he has been a good husband and a good father. We have lived in strange places, and I have experienced things I would never even have dreamed about, but he has always been there to make the mysterious seem fun and exciting. The kids and grandchildren adore

him, and now, since he is retired, he finds time for all of them. He likes to make toys and cook.

He is still fun and entertaining, but the gospel isn't something he thinks about except to cast negatives if I approach him about it in a way he doesn't like. I try to talk to God about him, not with him.

How do I cope? How do I maintain my relationship with him in spite of his attitude? I do my best to live the gospel. The thought of becoming inactive has never occurred to me. I attend church and accept callings as they come. I try to magnify my callings. I work in the temple now, and I am collecting our family history as a legacy for our children. I think faith, prayer, and hope never ceasing are the keys. These are gifts I have received, and no matter how indifferent and sarcastic he may be occasionally about the Church, I can step around him because I know he has a good heart. I read Church literature, and I try to live the gospel in every corner of my life. I know he has always seen that, and I know too that if the children and I ever wavered in our Church commitment, he would be the first one to scold us back onto the right track. Strange, isn't it? Still, I know he is the one I am to be with for all time and eternity.

My friend has learned to seek the Lord's constant counsel through the Holy Ghost. She told me that she has learned when to speak and when to be silent, when to encourage and when to let him find his own way. She said that in the very act of accommodating his resistant spirit, she has empowered the Holy Ghost to act in her life. She is learning wisdom. Phillip R. Kunz, a professor of sociology at Brigham Young University, suggested that in cases like this, "the first thing we should do is seek the Lord's help through fasting and prayer. . . . Prayer and meditation may bring about the inspiration of 'the right words,' or behavior that will influence the inactive one" ("I Have a Question," *Ensign*, April 1978, 40).

Elder Boyd K. Packer, in an address "to the Relief Society sisters whose husbands are not at present active in the Church or are not yet members of the Church" reminded us to never to give up. "Remember . . . that the home and the family are a unit of the Church. . . . If your husband doesn't feel at home going to church, then do everything you can to make him feel at church while he's at home" ("Begin Where You Are—At Home," *Ensign*, February 1972, 69, 70–71). I have tried through prayer and following the counsel of my leaders to keep my husband happy and content in our home. As Elder Packer said, "He needs to know, he needs to be told that you care about the gospel as deeply as you do and that you care about him infinitely more because of the gospel and what it means to you. Let him know that your goodness as a wife and as a mother, as a sweetheart and as a companion in love, grows from your testimony of the gospel" (ibid., 73). It took me some years to *really* understand this counsel.

In the relationship with my husband, I have learned that letting him practice his agency according to "the dictates of his conscience" is the way to keep the peace between us. When we were baptized and subsequently sealed as a family, he had not yet been converted. It has been important for me to remember that when we married, he did not marry a Mormon girl. He married a Protestant with a background similar to his own socially, economically, and even politically.

Suddenly, with my sincere conversion, he was presented with this beloved wife whose belief system and approach to life had been almost entirely altered. Where I had been "good" before, my hope was to become "better." Where I had given offerings before, nothing less than a tithe would satisfy my conscience. Where I had worn sleeveless dresses and blouses, nothing but definite sleeves and longer skirts was comfortable. No more two-piece swimming suits, no more shopping for anything on the Sabbath, and no more iced tea in the summer and hot tea in the winter. No more lazy Sundays.

Over time, these issues have faded to nothingness, and my husband, like my friend's husband, expects me to live my religion to the best of my understanding and ability. I respect the vast majority of choices my husband makes. He, too, is a good man who loves his wife and children. He is content in his work and spends a good deal of his leisure time gardening or working on home improvement projects. I try to remember, as one convert to the Church put it, "the gospel is perfect; people are not" (Sherry Fenton, in "Becoming Part of the Fold," *Ensign*, June 1999, 62). I suppose we have reached a time in our lives when we recognize that neither of us is perfect.

In her helpful and enlightening book, *Confronting the Myth of Self-Esteem*, Ester Rasband wrote:

> God's love is perfect, but we are not. Things of the world which we ignorantly would prefer as an expression of love may not be for our best good. They may even be destructive and therefore would not be an expression of love at all. We must be so humble that we trust the way our perfect Father in Heaven expresses his love for us and be grateful for it without condition. If we don't do that, if we are unwilling to receive it, we fail to collect it. Unrecognized and therefore uncollected, the love does not strengthen us, does not energize us, does not bless us (61).

One of my favorite hymns, "Come, Thou Fount of Every Blessing," reminds us: "O to grace how great a debtor Daily I'm constrained to be! Let thy goodness, as a fetter, Bind my wandering heart to thee" (*Hymns*, 1948, no. 70). Nephi's brother Jacob taught us to "remember, after ye are reconciled unto God, that it is only in and through the grace of God that ye are saved" (2 Nephi 10:24).

I am grateful for my challenges in mortality. For many years, I could not say that honestly. I simply did not understand; yet, even then, I didn't feel like blaming God for having an inactive husband. I joined the Church because I believed in Christ, in the Book of Mormon, and in the Restoration. I really didn't do it for anyone but myself, and it seemed, truly, like I was answering a call. With my baptismal covenants, I took upon myself eternal responsibilities for my family and for myself. I know now that mortality is a training and proving ground. This is the last big test, and if we do well, we can return to the presence of our beloved Father. He loves us and our spouses more than any of us can comprehend, and we owe him the allegiance that goodness deserves.

Calling ourselves Latter-day Saints means that we "should come unto Christ, who is the Holy One of Israel, and partake of his salvation, and the power of his redemption. Yea, come unto him, and offer your whole souls as an offering unto him, and continue in fasting and praying, and endure to the end; and as the Lord liveth ye will be saved" (Omni 1:26).

As we endure, he pours his compassion on us through the Holy Ghost and teaches us to endure well.

Unintentional Hurts

There are painful, sometimes even hurtful, circumstances that occur outside of the home as a consequence of having an inactive or less-active spouse. Although the attitudes seen in this next story are not always typical, the account illustrates the need to be aware of and reach out to those ward members who are struggling with inactive spouses:

> My point of view comes from living on both sides of this issue. For seven years I had a husband who was a seminary teacher, a member of the elders quorum presidency, and a member of the stake missionary presidency. Now, for ten years, I have had the

same man who has become an almost totally inactive member. A family's connection with a ward is through the priesthood holder. This is how the family gets information, learns of service projects, learns of other families, and is welcomed. A bishop knows about each family through the head of the household or priesthood leader.

It has been my experience that when the priesthood holder does not attend or hold a calling, the family is cut off from all the above. The family also is not invited to socialize with other families, and their children are not offered rides to Church functions, even when ward members live within the neighborhood. The family rarely has home teachers. This happens even if this family attends faithfully every Sunday. In our family, one child even attends BYU and I hold callings and a temple recommend. The family is considered not okay by most of the ward members, including the bishopric.

Example: I attended the Boise temple as a youth leader to do baptisms for the dead. My son also attended. As we were waiting in the waiting room, my bishop of six months pulled me aside and asked me if I had a temple recommend. I have lived in the same ward as this current bishop for fifteen years, but he did not know. Why would he wonder if I did or didn't? I think it was because my husband is not active, and that caused a double hurt.

I believe it would serve all of us well to be aware of the struggles of those around us. It is not easy to live the gospel in a divided household.

One young father I know has been left with the responsibility of raising three young children without the help of his wife. She left him and the family a few years ago. She has the children part of the time, but they are mostly with their father. He attends church, and he takes the children, but he also spends many Sundays at home or taking the children on hikes or other activities. He said:

I know we should be in Church, but it is really hard to get them [the children] ready to go. It is hard to keep track of them when we are there.

The whole thing is just too hard. People at church find fault with me for not getting the kids there every Sunday, but I don't see anyone reaching out to help us. Maybe it will be easier when they are older.

In a BYU Women's Conference address, Janet Scharman spoke of our everyday struggles as mortals on this earth. She said: "Problems arise, not always because of someone's mistake, or anyone's intention to hurt, or because our Heavenly Father has forgotten we are here. They are just part of living in an imperfect world. We have been given guidelines and commandments, which, if followed, will in the end result in our happiness. Because we can't always see the end from the beginning, we need to trust in what we do know and be willing to proceed with faith. When we are willing to do that, the next time we have a challenge, it becomes easier, and then even easier again" ("Saved by Hope," in *The Arms of His Love*, 43).

Remembering these truths is the way to cope during the sometimes long wait for a beloved spouse to feel and accept the gospel. With quiet, prayerful patience, even the waiting can become a thing of beauty. We must remember to treat our loved ones as the Lord would have us treat them, with love unfeigned. We are to be a font to them, offering the sweet, cool, and refreshing blessings of Christ's love until they are ready to be bathed in the light of their own gospel understanding. In doing this, we invite the Holy Ghost to be present; we find peace of mind and are enveloped with the sense of well-being that comes from fully committed service to those we love.

chapter two

Wandering Children: Caring for Tender Spirits

My youngest son is not active in the Church at the moment. He is well educated, hardworking, and kind-hearted, and I know that the time will come when he will remember what he was taught about the gospel in his youth at home and in the Church. For now, like his father, he has chosen to live a good life separate from Church activity. Over the years of his inactivity in the Church, people have often said to me, "Well, think of Heavenly Father, he lost a third." If those words are meant to comfort, I must say that they don't. It saddens me to reflect on the initial anguish our Heavenly Father and Mother must have felt when Lucifer and his followers were cast out. Unrestrained comments like that are painful to faithful members who live in hope that the difficult burden will be lifted and that beloved children will turn their hearts to their Heavenly Father. My son is not "cast out." He is not "lost." He is distracted. His heart is good; he has a mother, sisters, and a brother who pray for him with the faith of the believing; his name is often entered on the temple prayer roll. This son was born under the covenant I made long ago with my Heavenly Father, and the promise was that as long as I am worthy, the sealing will not be broken.

In a general conference of the Church held in April 1929, Apostle Orson F. Whitney stated:

> The Prophet Joseph Smith declared—and he never taught
> more comforting doctrine—that the eternal sealings of faithful

parents and the divine promises made to them for valiant service in the Cause of Truth, would save not only themselves but likewise their posterity. Though some of the sheep may wander, the eye of the Shepherd is upon them, and sooner or later they will feel the tentacles of Divine Providence reaching out after them and drawing them back to the fold. Either in this life or in the life to come, they will return. They will have to pay their debt to justice; they will suffer for their sins; and may tread a thorny path; but if it leads them at last, like the penitent Prodigal, to a loving and forgiving father's heart and home, the painful experience will not have been in vain. Pray for your careless and disobedient children; hold on to them with your faith. Hope on, trust on, till you see the salvation of God.

Who are these straying sheep—these wayward sons and daughters? They are children of the Covenant, heirs to the promises, and have received, if baptized, the gift of the Holy Ghost, which makes manifest the things of God. Could all that go for naught? (in Conference Report, April 1929, 110–11).

We are stewards, custodians of these children for a period of time; their spirits belong to our Heavenly Father. They may be sealed to us eternally as part of our families, but they have their own moral agency. We don't own them, but we promised not to let go of them entirely until they were on safe ground. It is hard, "But parents keep hoping," wrote Marvin Gardner in an August 1982 *Ensign* article. "And, reminiscent of three of the Lord's parables, they keep doing all they can to restore that which is lost. When the shepherd lost a lamb, he left his ninety and nine and scoured the hillsides relentlessly until he found it. When the woman with ten pieces of silver lost one piece, she lit a candle and swept the house until her search was fruitful. The father of the lost son had a more difficult task: respecting his son's agency, he stayed at home, waiting and watching, until the boy 'came to himself' and decided to return (see

Luke 15:4, 8, 11–20)" ("Keeping the Door Open and the Stew Hot: Loving and Helping a Wayward Child," 9).

Brother Gardner goes on to suggest that parents exercise charity, teach correct principles, build self-esteem, take time to listen, give the child or teenager room to breathe, never give up, and hope and pray.

The stories that follow show parents, mostly mothers, doing just these things. Some have the hoped-for resolutions, some are ongoing, some represent brief worries and struggles, and some represent serious, perhaps permanent losses of deeply loved children. Those who shared their successes and heartaches did so in the hope of comforting someone else. A sweet commonality among all of those I interviewed was a true sense of peace and hope. They were prayerful, positive-thinking people, although they openly admitted that sometimes sadness envelops them.

I reflected on their sadness, knowing well that familiar pain, and recalled the counsel of my mother: "When I am down, I allow three minutes to weep. Then, I get over it and give myself three hours to work hard and think it out. I have usually been able to pull myself up by that time, if not, well, three days is the longest sad-time I have ever allowed myself. I just pray all the while." In Doctrine and Covenants 136:29 we are advised, "If thou art sorrowful, call on the Lord thy God with supplication, that your souls may be joyful." I love that counsel. It works.

One of my closest friends had a son who became less active in the Church when he was in his early teens. He became involved in alcohol and drugs and eventually he began running with a gang. When she questioned him, or tried to restrict him, he became verbally abusive and stormed out of the house. Her husband was often away from home until late at night, and responsibility for the boy fell almost entirely to her. In recounting her story, she said:

> I am just an ordinary person, but I can tell you that I had to rely entirely on the Lord to help me survive [my son's] teenage years and then his long absence. When he was sixteen, he even demanded to go to a psychologist because he believed that his dad and I, because of our house rules, were abusive to him. We paid for counseling, but it didn't seem to help him understand or manage his rage. He would yell at me with such foul words that I would lock myself in the bathroom just to have a sense of safety. I would respond to him with the softest answers I could come up with, but he just continued yelling, evening after evening, and leaving the house. I prayed and cried and prayed some more.
>
> When he graduated from high school, we offered to pay for his university education. He refused to continue in school, and then he actually ran away. He took money from our home and disappeared on his motorcycle. We had no idea where he was for nearly two years. Then, close to Christmas, just after his twentieth birthday, he called and said that he was living in Pennsylvania and had just married. We were floored. He said he had a job that he liked and that his wife was in college there studying music.
>
> We began a new relationship from there. First we traveled to Pennsylvania to see him and to meet her. She was a gracious young woman, a Baptist, and a very fine pianist. We helped support them until she finished school, and then the company he was working for transferred them to Connecticut. They were both content to move there. She taught piano lessons in their home, and in just a few years they had three children. During a long phone call with me, she mentioned that they were not attending church but would like to begin because the children needed to learn about Jesus Christ.
>
> I thought about that and prayed about it and then decided to do something I had wanted to do for a long time. I asked the Lord

to take over. Soon, I found myself putting the names of their whole family on the temple roll, and then I made arrangements for the missionaries to visit their home. I said nothing about it, but somehow I knew this was what the Spirit was directing me to do. It was the exact time and the right thing to do. To make a long story short, she was baptized, he went through a period of repentance, and a few years ago they were sealed for all time and eternity in the Washington temple. Since then he has been transferred to Salt Lake City. We are a close family, and the past is a closed book.

One of the main things I learned from this was that responding with a soft answer, no matter what they say or yell, somehow binds their hearts to us so that they can turn back when they are ready. My son has told me many times that he always knew I loved him. It was critical for me to learn that the Lord doesn't expect us to do it alone. He expects the Holy Ghost to do it. If I could turn back the clock, I'd do things differently. I thought I was to call my son to repentance. It was tunnel vision.

I don't find this remarkable wife and mother "ordinary" all. She ultimately turned her heartache over to the Lord, and through the devotion of the missionaries, won her son back for Heavenly Father.

Holding on to Faith

Sometimes there are simply no easy resolutions to the anguish of a parent. I spoke with a grieving mother, now a single parent, who is enduring the suffering of a mentally ill child. She told me that she often feels self-doubt, and people no longer seem to remember her and the ongoing care she must give her beloved son. She wondered aloud, "How does the Atonement work in this? Where is the Lord?" She explained her son's need:

> My son has schizo-affective disorder. He has been ill since he was a young teenager, and now he is twenty-three. He needs love,

29

and he needs male models. He has been in and out of the hospital over the years, but it is as though he has been put outside the boundaries of "carrying each other's burdens." It is as though no one remembers him except his five siblings and me, and most of them live out of town.

I look at his suffering, and I wonder what we are supposed to be learning from this experience. Jesus Christ ministered three years, suffered physically for three days, and then it was over. My son is in a permanent state of fear and paranoia, and, added to that, we feel like victims of others' misunderstanding. Though he was bullied by neighborhood boys, he was never mistreated or abused at home; he was never neglected or abandoned. He is mentally ill, and it is as though people think it is somehow my fault.

I am so grateful for all of my children, and I am grateful to share their life journeys with them. It is lucky for me that I can see the way they live their lives and how they love one another, care about each other, and simply like each other. Yet, inside of me there is a core of sadness that doesn't seem to heal. My own health has deteriorated. My son is in the hospital again, but no one from the ward visits him, not even the home teachers or the bishop. It is as though they have forgotten or are afraid.

Elder Alexander B. Morrison, an emeritus member of the First Quorum of the Seventy reminds us: "Myths and misconceptions about the causation, course and treatment of mental illness unfortunately are found among Latter-day Saints as they are in the general public. These harmful and destructive attitudes include [many myths and misconceptions]. . . . As victims, loved ones, and all the rest of us increase our understanding, patience, forgiveness and empathy will replace denial, anger and rejection" ("Some Myths and Misconceptions about Mental Illness," 2, 3).

As members of ward families we must remember to seek out, support, and care for every member of the ward, visible or not.

Surely we can do a better job of caring for the parents of children with severe, ongoing disabilities. Those parents wear down and wear out. They need sustained help, and it is through us that the Lord gives that help. There is great peace of mind for the suffering to give service to those who suffer.

Helping Hands

The opportunity to help others regain or stay in the gospel path can come in less dramatic ways as well. Recently, I interviewed a mother of several children, many fully-grown and all active members of the Church. I asked if she and her husband had ever had any children who went astray even for a little while. She laughed and said that the Lord had sent very easy children for them to raise. She said that she prayed, took everyone to church, and tried to put out fires when they happened to flare. Still, she was grateful for the help of others in keeping her children active in the Church. She recalled one instance when her prayers for a child were answered in the actions of others:

> One of my boys was small for his age and very late with the onset of puberty. He was having some seriously negative feelings about himself, and the boys he had always been friends with kind of dropped him. He looked so much younger then they did in their early teens; I guess they didn't want him around. Most of them were not LDS boys; we lived in a small town in Indiana and there were very few members of the Church there. I prayed about it long and hard. I didn't want him to feel so bad. A few times he said he didn't want to go to church. He really didn't threaten to leave the Church, but he was uncomfortable even passing the sacrament because he felt different than the other boys who were there. I didn't want to lose him, but there didn't seem to be any way I could "fix it." Then, some missionaries in our area came

over for dinner one evening. That was the beginning of the end of that bonfire!

My son delighted in the missionaries, and I just started having them over pretty regularly. If they were in our area on Sunday, our son would sit with them. They even helped us move when we were transferred to the West. I don't feel like I really did anything much except welcome them into our home. Yet, they were a big part of the reason that our son got through that time in his life when he felt so unhappy.

At a missionary's farewell in northern Idaho, another mother recounted a story of simple, steady actions that kept her boy on the gospel path:

When it was time for him to be baptized, his father and I had just separated. His father was also estranged from the Church and saying some pretty bad things about it. I wanted him to be baptized and went to the bishop. The bishop advised me to wait, and so I did. We continued attending Church together regularly and living the gospel principles at home. My husband and I did divorce, but in less than a year, our son told me that he had changed his mind and wanted to be baptized after all. He loves his dad, and they have always been close, but his decision to be baptized was his own and he has never shown any further inclination not to live the gospel. He is so excited about the mission, and I know that he will be a good missionary. His father has never come back to the Church, but I hope having a son on a mission will have a good influence on him.

A student at BYU shared a story that shows the influence of brotherly love and patience. This student had a younger brother who was headed in the wrong direction. The family lived on the West Coast, and the student invited his younger brother to live with him in Provo. The older brother recounted how he extended a hand of loving friendship:

My brother is really a sensitive person. He thinks about things, and he writes poetry. I feel really positive about him, but I don't think he believes there is a God right now. He has had a lot of bad influences on him. He had a Scoutmaster who introduced him to some pretty bad things; his best friend was hit by a car and killed just after receiving his mission call; he has a twin and always feels compared to him; his girlfriend was not a good influence; he couldn't get a job at home and had no money to go to school.

He has gone back home now, and I am not really sure what I did for him. I provided food for him, but I never felt he was a burden. We played a lot of chess and basketball. Really, we had a lot of fun together. I was never embarrassed by him, even though he dressed his own way. I took him to an accounting dinner once, and I told him I didn't care what he wore. There are always many couples at those things, so I introduced him as my spouse and we had a lot of laughs from that.

He worries about being hypocritical. He wonders if people do things they really don't want to do for God. One day, he just left without notice. He left a note on the desk, left his stuff (a gym key and backpack), and I heard from him a day and a half later. He had driven back to the coast. He is nervous and had a stomachache as he left, but he asked one of my roommates for a Book of Mormon before he left, and he said: "Wouldn't my family be surprised if I would go on a mission?" I felt so happy when I heard he said that.

He is at home. Our mom says that he has really changed in many ways, and she is really grateful to me. I'm not sure what I may have done, but I am glad if his being here for a while relieved her burden.

He is working regularly now, living at home, and not causing anyone any trouble. We all hope that he will go back to Church, but we are just waiting.

A brother's unconditional love helped both a worried parent and an unsettled young man gain a little perspective.

Christ Knows His Sheep

The eye of the Shepherd is upon even children who have not been seen by their family for many years. A dear mother who lives in the eastern United States was widowed many years ago and left with six children to raise. All but the youngest son are active Church members and have married. Her deep concern continues for the youngest one, who left home to live in New York City almost ten years ago. He dropped all ties with the family. He had no known address or telephone number. He had never had a regular job in New York, but as a highly skilled computer technician he did temporary work in downtown Manhattan.

When I interviewed this mother, the young man was feared to have been lost in the World Trade Center attack. "With the tragedy of September 11, 2001," she said, "I will always wonder if he was there that day. He hasn't called for years, and until I hear from him, I will never know." With deep faith she said:

> I have to leave him in the hands of the Lord, and I have found that I can do that. I had to let go of the pain of his absence from the family a long time ago. Yet, with the terrorist attack, the whole wound opened again for the entire family. I was mesmerized for a time, just glued to the television hoping to catch a glimpse of him. I hurt, but I will heal again. We all just wish that he would have the decency to call if he is able, but we know that the Lord knows him, knows how he is and where he is, and loves him.

The son did call, at last, but I ache for this mother whose son doesn't seem to understand how much his family cares about him. For this mother there is a void that cannot be filled—a more and more common experience in this world of confusion and topsy-turvy values. To stay lovingly in touch with those who have drifted from Church activity is one of the key ways to make their return easier. Communication is a two-way choice, but by using technology, we are often able to stay in touch more easily with our loved ones. With each contact, tiny sparks of affection are fanned again and have the potential to grow into a glowing testimony of the gospel.

chapter three

In-Laws and Grandparents: Strengthening the Roots

For each recently baptized adult convert, a whole family is newly connected to the Church. Most, if not all, of that family are nonmembers, and most, if not all, know little or nothing about The Church of Jesus Christ of Latter-day Saints beyond the most general information. Some listen to the Tabernacle Choir, some have heard of or have even been helped by humanitarian efforts of the Church. Some have heard negative stories; some have hostile feelings and attitudes toward the Church and its members based on rumor and misrepresented information. My own father, as benign as he was toward my religious choices, thought that many Mormon bishops had several wives.

Young couples who join the Church, some accompanied by their young children, need continued relationships with their parents and the grandparents of their children. Catherine and Joseph Garcia-Prats remind us in their book *Good Families Don't Just Happen* of the treasure of grandparents and the importance of these ongoing relationships:

> As our family grew, it logistically became easier for the grandparents to visit Houston. We encourage these visits and love to see their relationships with our sons flourish. Papa Musco's trips to Shipley's Donuts are a welcomed treat. Grandma Musco's suitcase full of goodies makes it Christmas whenever she comes. Grandma Garcia always brings a new game or two to enliven an already lively house. And Grandpa Garcia thoroughly enjoys

talking with the boys about their latest adventures. The boys are blessed with special grandparent memories. Grandparents enrich children's lives and the unique grandparent-grandchild relationship helps young people appreciate the elderly, whether in their own families or in society.

David wrote an essay on grandparents in a seventh-grade creative writing class. He wrote: "When grandparents are near, there always seems to be excitement and joy. They are there when I need them. When my grandparents come to town, it's like rags to riches at our house. They spoil us, but I don't mind. My family seems closer together. They are the missing piece that makes our family one" (172).

One morning during the weeks my husband and I were taking the missionary lessons, my husband's father dropped by our house unexpectedly. He came in, sat on the edge of the couch in the living room, and said, "Jackie, do you know what you are doing with this church thing?"

"Yes," I said. "I think so."

"No, I don't think you do. Do you realize what this will do to the family socially?"

"No, I hadn't thought about that at all," I said. I was puzzled. I hadn't ever contemplated social status beyond being glad that our engagement and wedding pictures had been printed in the St. Louis Post-Dispatch because a lot of people knew our families. Two of my husband's uncles had been well-respected and widely known optometrists in the St. Louis area, and one of my uncles, a lawyer, had been a local mayor.

"Well, it is not good. Jackie, you don't need this church. The Methodist church is a good church, so is the Presbyterian."

I really didn't know what to say. I had deep regard for Dad Thursby. He had introduced my husband and me. After high school, while attending Washington University part time, I worked at an insurance company where Mr. Thursby was one of the vice presidents. After we became acquainted, he arranged the first date between his only son and me. I silently whispered a plea for help from Heavenly Father and said, "I have been to both of those churches, and as far as I am concerned they are good, but not what I want for our children. I'll tell you what, when you can show me something better, really better for the children than what I am finding here, I'll change churches. But until then, the children and Denny and I will go to the Mormon church."

He studied me for a while, stood up, and then said, "I guess you have made up your mind."

I stood up and said, gently, "Yes, I have." He then told me that he and Den's mother loved us very, very much and would always love us. I assured him that we felt the same way, and then he left.

Over the years our children were close to them, and we maintained close, supportive ties.

They helped us occasionally with the children, and as they grew older we assisted them in many ways. We remained a loving family, but after the day Dad Thursby visited with me, religion was seldom mentioned except for discussions about the reality of life after death. On that topic, Dad Thursby wanted to believe that there was continued life of the spirit, but he said that he just couldn't be sure.

Some months after Denny's father died, I was driving alone between errands and stopped at a stop sign. I wasn't thinking about anything particular when I heard a soft voice say simply: "Jackie, this is all right." It was Dad Thursby's voice. I was baffled for a moment, but then I felt the wonderful warmth that assured me of the steady presence of the Holy Ghost. Somehow I was impressed that Dad Thursby had let me know that his life had continued and that he was safe and happy. I have had his temple work performed, and I have always felt a sense of peacefulness when I think of him.

My mother's response to our joining the Church was not so civil. As I said, she came from a strong Southern Baptist heritage and, for starters, believed literally in the inerrancy of the scriptures. As a consequence, she believed (and still believes) that no current revelation is possible; therefore, no Book of Mormon or any other scriptures beyond the Old and New Testaments is valid. Her list of objections was long and included the question, "How in the world could you believe this nonsense when you have been as carefully taught as you have?"

My dad, a quiet, contemplative man, walked in on one of these heated lectures and, to my surprise, rescued me.

"What's going on?" he asked.

"She wants to be a Mormon," Mom said.

"So what?"

"Well, it is wrong. She can't do that." Mom was in tears. I was in tears. The children were watching and wondering, and everyone fell silent. Then my dad said, "Nadine, if Jackie wants this, let her have it. She is a Christian, and the children will be raised in a Christian church. Let it alone."

My dad died in 1991, and I have had his temple work done. The only LDS material he ever read was a biography of Orrin Porter Rockwell that I gave him for Christmas one year. He told me once that if mother were not so opposed, he might "sit through a round of missionary lessons." Mother's attitude has never changed, but I feel that my dad has accepted the gospel, and sometimes I have a sense that he is very close.

It would be unfair to my mother if I didn't also mention the tremendous influence for good that she and my father have had on our children. My parents liked the beautiful outdoors of Missouri. They had a modest cabin about eighty miles from St. Louis, and on every possible occasion took one or all of our children for weekends there. This was a complicated situation because if the children went to the country, which they all loved to do, it meant missing church.

On weekends during the winter, Mother would invite us for Sunday dinner, but that often conflicted with our afternoon sacrament meeting. Sometimes I could negotiate the times with her, but it was a point of tension. She clearly expressed her view that it was ridiculous for our church to have a meeting on Sunday afternoon. The Baptists meet on Sunday morning and Sunday evening. For us, these conflicts were finally resolved when we accepted a transfer to Idaho offered by my husband's company.

To this day, my mother, now ninety-two, remains a rock of faith. She preaches the words of Christ to all of us from her solid Southern Baptist foundation, and she lets us all know that we are in her prayers constantly. We have maintained good relationships over the years, and again, we have all learned not to try to discuss religious preferences.

The responses of extended family can vary from complete disavowal of family members who join the Church to continued growing relationships. One of my friends shared a story with me about her husband's family:

> My husband's parents divorced after his birth, and his mother remarried. His father did not stay in touch with the family. His mother, who died just a few years ago, left a good history of her side of the family, but my husband wanted to know more about his biological father and his heritage. All we knew was the name of a town his mother had mentioned a few times, but we did not know for sure if he still lived there.
>
> A few years ago, we took our children on a trip which took

us through that town. We looked in a local phone book, and to our amazement, his name was listed! We called, identified ourselves, and were warmly invited to his ranch to meet both him and his wife. Since then we have maintained a connection with them, though the communications from our side are more frequent towards them than theirs have been towards us. They have sent us a few notes and cards. We would like to teach them the gospel, and thought at first that they were interested, but they have let us know that they are not. What I think I have learned from this is that no matter if people we care about respond to the gospel or not, it is important to keep loving and to maintain contact even if there are few visible gospel results.

This is a kind and remarkable story. By putting the past behind, new links were established, and a family has been reunited in love. My friend told me that at first they were wary because they didn't know this man or his wife. But he was so enthusiastic about meeting all of them and he so fully embraced the idea of having grandchildren that trust was quickly established and past regrets were largely buried. New dimensions of their family history have been found, and the son is hopeful that someday he will be able to help his father and stepmother learn the gospel.

Another of the women I interviewed discussed the strain of maintaining good relations with her family when she was first married. She told me that she had been raised as a Lutheran and had been conservatively educated in Lutheran parochial schools. She reached a point in her late teens when she felt something was missing and desired to know more about God. During that time she met her husband, a Latter-day Saint and returned missionary. They were both students at the University of Michigan and had a psychology class together. One afternoon he invited her to go for a snack on campus, and they began to explore ideas that had been discussed in class. That discussion led to a serious exploration of one another's beliefs.

As she told it:

> It wasn't long before he asked me what I now know are the "Golden Questions." I did want to know more. The missionaries came to my apartment and two of my friends took the discussions with me. Neither of them were able to accept the message, but it felt correct to me, and I was baptized about five weeks after first encountering my someday-to-be husband in the class.
>
> I have never had any problem in the conversion from Lutheran to Latter-day Saint except having to modify some of my holiday traditions, but it was a difficult thing for my parents to accept the change in me and the adjustment in our way of celebrating holidays. Our family has been Lutheran for many generations, and there were traditions that were and still are a part of our family way of doing things.
>
> In my family, the period of Lent was a time of quiet meditation and more frequent attendance at church. On the day before Easter, we always had a day of preparation for the Easter egg hunt which took place early on Easter morning. We usually looked forward to new spring clothes which we wore first on Easter Sunday. His family, on the other hand, had a family get-together, often a picnic (modified to an indoor dinner if the weather was bad), and the Easter church services were just like any other Sunday. My extended family understood that I was still a Christian, but they never have understood our different way of celebrating Christmas and Easter.
>
> To them, these were the high holy days of the Christian calendar; to me, after my conversion, they were important days, but not so . . . unique as they had been before.

She told me that it was through negotiation and prayer that bridges were built between her and her Lutheran parents, brothers, and sisters. They are all in frequent contact, and good feelings permeate the family. The cousins know and love each other, but religion is seldom a topic of discussion. Weddings, graduations, baby blessings or christenings, holidays, and funerals call for frequent trips and associations, and the family moves on in love and good will in spite of "our Mormon peculiarity," as she put it, explaining, "We practice mutual respect, and the family, though still Lutheran, has a pretty clear view of what we believe and practice. The most important part to them is that they know we are Christians."

Reflecting on Denny's and my first experiences in the Church, I can remember the way our families reacted to our associations as new members in the mid-1960s. We were fellowshipped warmly by young couples in our ward.

A year and a few months after our baptism, a year of truly joyful anticipation, we took the train to Salt Lake City and were met there by former St. Louisans who greeted us warmly and provided a place to stay. We were "married" again there and then sealed as a family in the Salt Lake Temple. One of the officiators there remarked to Denny, "I can hardly believe you are a convert. You look just like a wholesome Latter-day Saint!" That was and is true. Denny was the picture of goodness. I was so thankful that my prayers had been answered and that our family had been sealed with authority and all the blessings of the priesthood for all time and eternity.

My parents, particularly my mother, thought this whole procedure was an expensive and inconvenient waste of time. This attitude repeated itself as a pronounced conflict when our daughter married in the Logan temple, and neither my parents, nor my husband's mother, widowed by then, could witness the sealing ceremony. There were calm explanations, and I gave them materials to read about temple weddings. My parents traveled from St. Louis and waited in a restaurant outside of the temple grounds during the ceremony. My husband's mother and his sister waited in the temple waiting room with my husband, who had long ago let his temple recommend expire. I know they didn't understand, but his mother and sister were gracious about it.

Some years later, an uncle of my husband and his wife visited our home in Idaho. During their visit, the uncle let me know how much it had hurt my husband's mother not to have been able to enter the temple and witness the sealing ceremony. He made it clear that he thought we were very out of line in our rules and regulations concerning temples, and said he had little use for Mormons in general. My husband and I remained courteous, but felt a sense of relief when their visit finally ended.

Not long after that, I called Mom Thursby and said that I was sorry she had felt that way but I did not know what I could do about it. She told me that it had been very hard at the time but that she seldom thought about it anymore. She was so pleased that her granddaughter and her husband were happy, and that was all that really mattered.

Celestial marriage puts us on the path leading to the highest of three heavens within the celestial world (see D&C 131:1–4), but it isn't difficult to understand, I think, how hard it is for those who have not learned these principles to accept what seems to be exclusionary and privileged.

One afternoon I chanced to meet one of the members of our stake presidency, also a BYU professor. He asked me how things were going in our family, and I said that there is progress but it is not as speedy as I would like. He asked, "Are you doing your genealogy work?" I was surprised, and I said that I had managed to get the work done for several family members on both sides, my husband's and mine, that year.

He said, "Good. Stick with it. You need the prayers of your converted dead to help you in the battle you are waging with Satan for your family."

I have reflected on his words many times. Not long after, when I did the temple work for my husband's mother, I was filled with joy and hopefulness in the temple. It was an interesting, faith-promoting experience, both unusual and sweet but clear and easy to understand. One of the temple workers noticed that the name Thursby was repeated several times on the ordinance card. I explained that I was doing the work that day for my beloved mother-in-law. The sister looked at me and then said, "I hope that something occurs in the temple this day to assure you that she has accepted the message." I went on to the chapel to wait for the endowment session to begin. For the first time since 1967—when my husband and I had acted as the witness couple and then were sealed later that day—I was invited to serve as the female in the witness couple, along with a volunteer male missionary. It was during that experience that I felt the presence of my husband's parents so strongly.

As I have stated before, I was close to them for all the years I knew them. I felt the assurance that they were present, and that my mother-in-law accepted the work done in her behalf. A few weeks later I participated in their sealing to one another. I believe my husband's parents will help me in the prayers for their beloved only son. I believe efforts like these will help all of us to retrieve our loved ones and become united families for all time and eternity.

chapter four

Relationships with Extended Family Members

Poignant recordings of cell phone calls made on September 11, 2001, again reminded the whole world that the most valuable and precious relationships are those shared by family members. After the tragedy, there was an upward swing in church attendance and voluntarism in the United States. A national soberness, sort of a shared civil religion, seems to have awakened in many who were caught up in everyday life. People of all nationalities and religions are working together even more conscientiously to create the united and respectful society many have prayed for, worked for, and hoped to establish for decades.

A good friend who lives in Salt Lake City shared the following story with me. Her father's half brother had drifted away from the family and the Church. He found a place to live in California. Several years ago, my friend had an impression that she should write this uncle. Most of the family had stopped trying to communicate with him, but they did have his address. She sent him pictures of her children, newsy notes about the family, and yearly holiday greetings. He never wrote back. A few years ago he died, and the family was contacted. His landlady, who had become his good friend and caretaker over the years, sent the accumulated cards, pictures, and notes back to Utah to the return address. With them, she enclosed a note of thanks and said that whenever he received a piece of mail, he referred to this niece as "my dear baby girl." In his illness, he did not acknowledge the receipt of the many thoughtful mailings, yet his simple words conveyed by the landlady validated the powerful family love that was transmitted to him through this kind niece. Since that time, my friend's son has performed the temple work for this uncle with the hope that he will be turned back to the gospel on the other side.

Elder Neal A. Maxwell gave many insights for strengthening families: "After all, mortal families predate the founding of nations, and families will exist after the Almighty 'hath made a full end of all nations' (D&C 87:6). . . . As Latter-day Saints, we need to do better in our families—much better! There should be less wringing of hands and more loving arms around our families" ("Take Especial Care of Your Family," *Ensign*, May 1994, 89).

In The Church of Jesus Christ of Latter-day Saints, we are taught that family ties are meant to last through all eternity. The Church organization is a temporary vehicle for the administration of the gospel ordinances; the family is the eternal unit. How can we continue to have close family ties when philosophical and religious views vary so widely? How can we avoid friction when points of view can differ so dramatically?

One key to healthy, functional family relationships is respect. Combine the respect with interest and consistency, and all family members can be helped to feel part of a larger whole. Forgiveness is another key. Most of us know how tensions can develop at holidays or in other family settings when old hurts, embarrassments, or bygone errors and differences are brought up. "Letting go" is an easy concept to understand but a difficult one to put into practice. If we intend to establish close family links, lasting links, across the boundaries of different belief systems and philosophies, then we must learn when to speak and when to remain silent. We must learn when to let go, and when to respect a different viewpoint.

There are many ways to bridge old hurts and provide renewed relationships with the extended family.

Our Ecumenical Family

In our extended family there are at least ten different religions: Southern Baptists, Northern Baptists, Presbyterians, Methodists, "Son" Fundamentalists, Lutherans, Catholics, Congregationalists, Unitarians, and Latter-day Saints. My children have close Jewish friends, and my husband and I have many friends and relatives who claim no religion at all. The most vigorously proselytizing group among us is my husband's sister, whose fundamentalist views openly declare that the rest of us are morbidly and eternally confused in our various religious persuasions. We love the fundamentalists, along with everyone else, but try to avoid discussing religion when we are together.

Not long ago, Anna, the four-year-old granddaughter of my husband's sister, was diagnosed with acute juvenile leukemia. She is slowly recovering, but her treatment was complex, painful, and frightening. Over the course of Anna's illness, many lives were touched, and family members in various branches of the family—people Anna will probably never meet—cared for her, asked about her, and prayed for her. I put her name on the temple prayer roll many times. My mother still prays daily for Anna's positive response to the treatments and for her complete recovery. My children and their families have prayed for her. My husband's sisters and their families have remembered her. Anna has become a part of her whole extended family, and she has become a focus of broad family caring. There will never again be a time in our extended family that Anna is forgotten; her illness brought us together in a unique way, and we discovered at a new level the faith and tender caring of one another.

49

Intolerance of religious differences can create tensions and mis-understandings that lurk for years under a facade of courtesy. Maturity and getting along with one another require honest self-evaluation, reflection, and forgiveness. Sometimes forgiveness doesn't occur instantly, but we should work towards it. In our family, like so many others, there are many memories. Some of those memories are grim, irritating, or embarrassing. People do grow and change, and everyone needs to try to remember (and allow) that. As Latter-day Saints we preach repentance and forgiveness. We, of all people, must practice what we have been taught by Jesus Christ; that is, to forgive and forget. Learning to leave the past, including immature decisions, in the past is an important part of respect and forgiveness.

I appreciated the advice given in a holiday article by Dr. Joyce Brothers called "Reconnect with Your Family." Her counsel was addressed to those who find that, even with the best intentions, family gatherings sometimes become a forum for remembered pains and competitions. Her tips for healing family conflict and thus making gatherings more meaningful and enjoyable included selecting a neutral, respected family mediator who could help family members meet and perhaps resolve their differences and begin their relationships anew.

Brothers suggested that a family hold a "Feast of Reconnection," which might include sharing of the food preparations and the clean-up. Other suggestions she made included bringing photographs to the gathering and sharing the past, asking "family genealogists to distribute copies of the family tree or recount family history" or having "the older generation . . . tell family stories as the young generation writes them down or records them with a tape recorder. By linking the two generations, you stress family continuity" (*Parade Magazine*, 4 November 2001, 6, 7). She also suggested considering ways to keep the family in contact after the holidays, such as creating a family Web page at one of the free sites available for that purpose. It is vital that we learn to forgive each other and get along well with our own families.

The family is the eternal unit of the gospel; and our families will be connected through all eternity if we work to bring them together. As we are reminded in Mosiah 27:31, in the end every knee will bend in acknowledgment of our Heavenly Father and the Savior, Jesus Christ. We cannot afford the nonsense of not valuing one another as we should. C. S. Lewis reminded us that if we really knew who we were, if we really recognized the nobility of each human with whom we came in contact, we would have to restrain ourselves from bowing down in worship (see *The Weight of Glory*, 45–46). I believe that, and as Latter-day Saints, I think you do too.

In a family where some have become members of The Church of Jesus Christ of Latter-day Saints, but most have not, it is particularly important for Church members to continue to foster good, or even excellent, relationships in the extended family. Elder Richard G. Scott said, "Where family or national traditions or customs conflict with the teachings of God, set them aside. Where traditions and customs are in harmony with His teachings, they should be cherished and followed to preserve your culture and heritage" ("Removing Barriers to Happiness," *Ensign*, May 1998, 87).

One of my acquaintances from Finland, a convert to the Church when in her late teens, told me of customs she has taught to her American husband and children, American relatives of other religions, and also friends who are not Latter-day Saints. She practices these traditions with the family during the Christmas season:

> We keep the old traditions and share them during the

holiday season. We try to keep Christmas like my parents kept it in Finland, but of course there are changes. We have a feast on Christmas Eve with baked ham, mashed potatoes, and applesauce. My children love smoked salmon. We use prunes in some of the desserts; our Joulutortut, or Christmas Prune Tarts, are filled with prune jam. We always have a gingerbread house that we eat! My parents liked to have herring and creamed cod, but we in America don't enjoy those so much. . . .

There is an old custom in Finland to go to the cemetery on Christmas Eve and put a candle on the grave of each loved one. We only have a few family members buried in the cemetery here, but we don't forget them. And even though we are Latter-day Saints, we have an Advent wreath and light candles each of the four Sundays before Christmas.

Our family and friends enjoy these traditions. They don't conflict with our beliefs as Latter-day Saints, and it is fun to be able to include family members and friends in all of our Finnish celebrations. Our home is filled with greens and candles at Christmas; we play and sing both Finnish and American Christmas songs; and we have a dance we do around the Christmas tree on Christmas Eve.

"When conceived in principles of righteousness, and when performed in a spirit of noncoercive participation, a heritage of family customs can serve as the social glue that holds families together, ushers family members through difficult life passages, and weaves loving ties of eternal duration" (Jill Rudy, Eric Eliason, and Kristie Bell, "Valuing, Preserving, and Transmitting Family Traditions," in David C. Dollahite, ed., *Strengthening Our Families*, 314). There are so many important traditions that can be shared despite religious differences. There are various points to consider when creating family traditions, and all of these can be adapted to help bridge differences. Some possibilities include the following:

1. *Distinguish between good and bad traditions:* Families should distinguish between traditions that reinforce gospel ideals and those that are not in harmony with gospel principles. . . .

2. *Encourage a unique family style:* . . . Children enjoy and remember these particular customs as part of their family and gospel heritage.

3. *Be selective and creative in fashioning new traditions:* When new families are formed by marriage, couples or parents should adapt old family traditions from both spouses. . . .

4. *Be inclusive:* . . . Take care to consider the variety of interests and abilities of all family members and choose inclusive activities that foster family relationships. . . .

5. *Be service oriented:* . . . Performing service as a family is one of the best ways to perform service within the family.

6. *Foster storytelling:* Knowing family history and stories is central to building healthy families with a strong sense of identity and values. . . .

7. *Nurture natural traditions:* Successful family traditions often grow out of things that the family already does (ibid., 314).

Sometimes we inadvertently discover interests among our extended family members that connect us in the deepest, most important ways. I have a nephew who is a devout Lutheran. He grew up close to our children and has warm friendships with each of them. One day I mentioned to him that I was the unofficial family genealogist. His eyes filled with tears, and he said: "I knew somebody in the family had to know something about our history. How much do you have? May I have copies? I have three kids, and I want them to know their roots. My mother doesn't know anything about her family; they were Italians, but they didn't keep records. I didn't know that you knew stuff about my dad's side. I am so excited!"

We are sending him information as we research it. To me, this is a step toward his understanding of the generations and their links.

Someday, through this connection, maybe he, his wife, and their children will be led to the truth of the gospel. Through our research over the last several decades, we have met family members that we would never have known otherwise. The turning of the "heart of the fathers to the children, and the heart of the children to their fathers" (Malachi 4:6) is an essential part of the gospel. Reach out to your family members to share what information you have. It is your heritage, and searching for roots has become a popular and satisfying hobby for many people who at this point have no apparent interest in the revealed purposes for the work. Use traditions and stories from your common heritage to unite your family and include everyone. Put "loving arms" around your extended family through your faith, service, celebrations, and family history.

chapter five

Friends: Patiently Sharing the Joy

Most of us have been blessed to have many good friends. Some, of course, are active Latter-day Saints. Others may be less active, be devout members of other churches, or attend no church at all. I have friends in all these situations who have taught me deep and beautiful principles of the gospel. There have been LDS friends who supported me during times when my husband has not wanted me to participate fully in Latter-day Saint Church activity, and non-LDS friends who have delighted in taking me to their churches when I was not participating in my own. Those, especially, were tender times for me. There have always been friends who have been willing to share their perceptions of spiritual life with me when I was longing for my own "comfort zone" but wanted also to explore the beliefs of others.

An Indian friend took me to a Jain Hindu ceremony and invited me to stay for the delicious Indian dinner afterwards. I met a Catholic nun in one of my classes in Toledo. She was a student from Brazil and invited me to her convent to attend Mass and then have a Sunday dinner with the nuns. She took me for a tour of the convent, and I returned to make handwoven crafts with the sisters. I have a dear friend who is Jewish and who has invited me to many services at the synagogue. Unitarian friends invited my husband and me to celebrate a mixed program at Christmastime; it was a beautifully blended celebration of Christmas, Kwanza, and Yoruba traditions.

When I am invited to attend church with others, I accept and go, much as I did as a child. In turn, when I invite my friends to activities in the ward or stake, they often accompany me. They are diverse and loving, and I try to stay in touch with all of them. I hope that on either this side or on the other side of the veil, they will understand and accept the restored gospel. In the meanwhile, it is my mission to love them and be the best friend I can be.

What is friendship, and how do we develop genuine friendships with people in and out of the Church? How do we bridge prejudice against Mormons? The prevailing philosophy inherent in those who volunteered at the 2002 Winter Olympics in Salt Lake City was friendliness and helpful support; during the two and a half weeks the Olympics came to Salt Lake City, Utah became internationally known by those attributes. The Olympics were safe, welcoming, and rewarding. Can genuine personal friendship be less than that? Based on trust, friendships validate our worth, affirm our feelings, and sift through our wheat and chaff. I've always been told that a person is lucky to have a few very close friends. I am very lucky then, because I trust many people and consider a host of human beings to be my very close friends.

One of my very close friends, Ursula, who now lives in Germany, goes to no church and believes in little she can't see, and yet she has often expressed how glad she is that I believe and am able practice my LDS faith.

Part of my academic work has included interviewing Basque women near the border of Spain and France and in the Western United States. Most Basques with whom I interacted believed in their priesthood and gospel with the same fervor and dedication as understanding Latter-day Saints. They value themselves and their families, and I respect them. My husband and I have been invited to many, many weddings, christenings, and funerals in the Catholic Church, and I have come to greatly admire their devotion to their ancient Catholic heritage and beliefs.

Susan is a long-time friend of mine who lives in Idaho. She is not LDS, nor does she ever intend to be. I met her when I was working on a research project in the West. She knew my beliefs, and early in our friendship she said:

> Now look, Jackie, I like you and all that, and Harry [her husband] and I enjoy having you and Denny over and going out together, but don't do any of your missionary numbers on us. I grew up in Salt Lake City, and I know what some of your people are up to.
>
> I am a Catholic, and so are my husband and children. I was educated in Catholic schools and then graduated from [a private university in Utah]. My children have really been marginalized by the predominant group in their high school here in Idaho, and they want no part of the Mormon church either. We will be sending them to Catholic colleges, and they will marry Catholic if they marry. We live our religion.
>
> I want this friendship, Jackie, but if I die before you, I'm warning you, don't get me baptized in one of your temples or I'll come back and haunt the daylights out of you!

She said this with a smile, but I knew she meant it. She and her family are Christians; they give freely of their time and means to their family, their church, and their community. I laughingly assured her there was no need to worry. I said, "Susan, everyone has a choice, permanently. You'll never have to join the Church, unless you want to."

Her rejoinder was, "I won't."

Though I couldn't promise Susan that I would never have her baptized vicariously, I did my best to assure her of her free choice, and we have never returned to the topic. I live my religion; she lives hers. She has attended Relief Society functions with me, and I have occasionally attended Mass with her. Now that we live far apart, we have maintained the friendship through phone calls, birthday and Christmas cards, occasional notes, and visits for weddings, funerals, and sometimes just fun.

Getting permission for the performance of vicarious baptism is not beyond the scope of genuine friendship, however. Elder Neal A. Maxwell once said: "One of the reasons we love each other in the Kingdom is that our friendships are not friendships of initiation at all, but are, instead, friendships of resumption" (in *Neal A. Maxwell Quote Book*, 132). When I was in second grade, my Brownie troop leader offered us the opportunity to establish pen pals with Girl Guides in England. I volunteered, and my "pen pal" was Valerie Ann of Leicestershire, England. I wish I had saved those early notes scrawled in childish script, but from the beginning we were fast friends. The correspondence continued through our elementary school years, on into high school, college, courting, marriage, and continued into our lives as young wives and mothers. We wrote monthly letters about our ups and downs, successes and failures, hopes and dreams for our husbands, children, and ourselves. I even named one of my daughters for her. When my husband had an audit to conduct in England and Scotland for his company, I was able to accompany him and finally meet my dear pen friend.

I stayed at her home for a week, participated in her life, met her immediate and extended family, shopped in her village, visited her son's school, and enjoyed myriad other experiences. Amazingly, we looked a little alike, laughed at the same things, and delighted in each other's presence. Valerie's mother remarked that it was "no surprise that the two of you are so alike. Otherwise, why would you have kept writing all of these years?"

I was taller than Valerie, but our coloring and even our tastes were much the same. As we were walking one day through a meadow in Stratford-on-Avon, where she took me to see Shakespeare's home, I remarked, "Oh, Val, these weeds are Queen Anne's lace; we have these at home but they grow larger." She smiled at me and said, "Oh, Jackie, not to offend, but everything American is bigger. You are bigger, your suitcase is bigger, and now, even your weeds are bigger!" We both laughed. In 1972, Valerie and her family traveled to the United States. With three of our four children, we met them in New York City and toured our way back to St. Louis by way of Niagara Falls, Philadelphia, Washington, D. C., and Williamsburg. We had a huge station wagon that accommodated all of us, but we took some teasing about the size of the car. There was teasing, too, about the extraordinary size and distances in America.

Val and I continued our monthly correspondence until there was an unusual lapse. After a few months, a letter came from England in an unfamiliar handwriting: Valerie had died suddenly. After a dinner party at her home, she had bid good-bye to her guests and was in the midst of the clean-up when she suffered a sudden, sharp pain in her upper back. A neighbor who was a doctor came quickly to her home and said he thought she was exhausted and needed a good night's rest. Twenty minutes after he left, Valerie died peacefully. She had had no previous heart problems; her left ventricle had suddenly collapsed. Her family was broken-hearted, and so was I.

About a year later, I dreamed of Valerie. She looked pretty in the dream, dressed in a red sweater and black skirt, colors she favored. She was sitting on a cement bench beside a huge, stone wall. The dream was vivid and stayed in my mind for days. Because I felt it was a message, I began to work toward getting her temple work done. Permission from her husband and parents was given in writing, because her family felt anything that would give me comfort would be all right with them. As I waited in the Logan Utah Temple to perform temple work on her behalf, a voice came into my mind that seemed to come from behind me. It was Valerie's voice with an unmistakable English Midlands accent. "Thank you, Jackie," she said. "Thank you very much."

I doubt I will have an opportunity like that for Susan (performing vicarious ordinances for friends is a rare opportunity in the first place), but I'm thankful for what I was able to do, and I'm looking forward to an eternal friendship with my dear friend Valerie. Her parents are now deceased, but her husband and son are still in touch with us each Christmas. So far, they have shown no interest in the Church, but I'll wait comfortably, knowing I have done what I could to help my friend. Elder Maxwell has said, "The finest of friends must sometimes be stern sentinels, who will insist that we become what we have the power to become. The 'no' of such stern sentinels is more to be prized than the 'yes' of others" (in *Maxwell Quote Book*, 132).

Applied Friendship

I watched a judge and his wife become genuine saviors to one of our dear friends who was being destroyed spiritually, mentally, emotionally, and physically by an abusive spouse. Their relationship had reached a point where her teenage son was sleeping with a ball bat under his bed to protect his mother, sisters, and himself. Earlene, my friend, was a devout LDS wife and mother, but though her less-active husband had promised to take her to the temple to be sealed, it had never happened. She was losing hope, and despite her strong testimony, she was finding it harder and harder to attend church regularly.

Earlene had been advised not to take out her own endowments until her marital situation improved, but one day she called me and said: "Jackie, I envy your ability to just take off and go to the temple for the day now and then. My husband would not like for me to do that, and it would mean another fight, I'm sure, but I have never been to the temple, and I want to go so much. He doesn't want me to go to church at all, nor does he want me to take the children anymore."

At the time I was doing a lot of temple work for my family, so I asked the stake president if there would be any way that Earlene could do some of the baptisms. He said, "Yes, absolutely. Have her go to her bishop and get a recommend, and she will be able to do both baptisms and confirmations."

Several times, Earlene and I traveled together to the temple, and she was able to help with the work and linger there to feel the Spirit and commune with the Lord. She resolved, on one of those temple trips, to take her children and leave her abusive husband, but she was afraid. She suffered two broken ribs and many bruises before our friend the judge and his wife literally rescued her.

Without Earlene's knowledge, the judge contacted her parents, who lived south of Logan, Utah, and they prepared their home to receive Earlene and her three children. Then, one morning after Earlene's husband had left for work, the judge and his wife pulled into her driveway with a pick-up truck and a trailer. They said, "Earlene, gather what you want from this house for your children and yourself because today you are moving."

She was frightened and crying, but she did as instructed, picked up the children from school on the way out of town, and that was that. She loved her less-active husband very much, but action was needed, and the judge and his wife were there to help. Soon after leaving her husband, Earlene received her endowments. After the divorce, Earlene began attending Church-sponsored dances, met a fine man, and was sealed to him in the temple. Recently, her children have been sealed to the two of them for all time and eternity, and Earlene is safe and happy.

Unintentional Neglect

I have friends, too, whose stories haven't turned out as well as Earlene's—friends who have fallen away from the Church because they lacked the friendship and support that they needed. A widowed mother and single adult daughter, Alice and Joyce, joined the Church some years ago in a Midwestern state and became very active in their ward. They had been disaffected Roman Catholics. The two of them liked to travel, but they had a little dog that did not travel well. I liked dogs, and so did my children. So, I volunteered us to serve as dog-sitters. This worked well for years until we moved to Idaho. They always paid me a little and brought small gifts to the children.

We corresponded for a few years after our family moved West, and then the correspondence became only notes at Christmas. At one point, Alice told me they felt left out of things in the ward. They wrote that they had a home teacher who never came and visiting teachers who were erratic. This mother and daughter seemed interested in what our family was doing, and they were positive with me but eventually wrote that they had quit attending church at all. In one of our last Christmas notes, Joyce wrote that Alice had become ill and had passed away. We continued the Christmas correspondence, and then one year my Christmas card was returned with the stamp "Unknown Address." Our family loved them and didn't want to lose touch. In trips back to the Midwest, I have tried to find Joyce's address, but so far I've been unsuccessful. It is hard for me to lose old friends, but I hope that somehow, somewhere, we will meet again.

Wilferd A. Peterson wrote: "To be a friend, a man should strive to lift people up, not cast them down; to encourage, not discourage; to set an example that will be an inspiration to others" (*Twenty-Three Essays on the Art of Living*, 30).

I have a friend named Margaret who has been that kind of a friend to me. Margaret is a devout Irish Catholic. (I think many of us limit ourselves by having friendships only "within the fold.") Margaret enriched my life immeasurably, and I am so thankful to have had the good fortune to live next door to her during the time I was in my doctoral program at Bowling Green State University in Ohio. She had been planning to sell her home, but stayed until we were ready to move back to the West. Margaret was widowed; her husband had been a microbiology professor, and she had a master's degree in library science. All of her seven children had graduated from college, and two of them had earned a Ph.D. For me, plowing though the Ph.D. program was a delightful but arduous, unfamiliar process. I was not young and doubted the sensibility of the work now and then. I was also ill for part of that time, and my father died of lung cancer during my first semester.

Margaret was a friend to me when I really needed a Christian friend. She was also an amazing example. She was trained in drama, and at one time she and her husband had toured the United States with a Shakespearean group. She read and recorded texts for the blind through a volunteer program in Toledo. She lived frugally and frequently traveled on a shoestring budget. Her home was lined with books. She cared for me; she listened when I needed it, and she understood. She encouraged me, and she set an example of refinement, education, and dignity. She has passed her seventieth birthday, and since she was sixty she has been taking classes at the University of Toledo for five dollars a class. After the classes, she tries to go to the countries she has studied. She is an intellectual, yet she bakes bread, cakes, and pies for friends and neighbors. She taught me to be patient in study, and coached me through the academic culture.

Margaret took us to her church, and we took her to ours. I could not and would not change her; she is devoted to her church. She was lonely in spite of her activities, and my husband and I happened to be "the needy new kids on the block." I think that someday she and her beloved husband will be together again for all time and eternity. One of her sons now lives in Salt Lake City, and we have been able to take her to dinner on her yearly Christmas trips to the West. What an experience we would have missed if we had been too busy to love and be loved by this delightful Irish Catholic!

Joseph Smith said, "Friendship is one of the grand fundamental principles of 'Mormonism'; [it is designed] to revolutionize and civilize the world, and cause wars and contentions to cease and men to become friends and brothers" (*Teachings of the Prophet Joseph Smith*, 316). Our friendships, whether with those who are active in the Church or active in no church, can enrich all our lives and give us all opportunities to live and share the gospel.

chapter six

Strengthening Our Family Ties

When the children were still at home, I planned and regularly held family home evening on Monday night. We read the scriptures together and we prayed together. Sometimes we played games, and sometimes we went out for an inexpensive supper and a movie. My patriarchal blessing prompted me to maintain our home as a "pleasing place where the Spirit of the Lord could be felt." I have been taught that if we did this regularly, our family would be together for all eternity.

If the scriptures were involved, Denny did not participate; but we would often have the religious part first and then play games or do something else he would enjoy. Sometimes we would invite friends of the children, mostly members of other churches, to participate. Our attitude was like that of many other successful families with a less-active parent: "If he joins us—great, we love to have him. But we just can't wait around for him, no matter how much we love him" (in "How to Cope: Father's Inactivity Doesn't Stop Family," *Church News*, 3 January 1981, 15). I taught the children that their father is a good man, regardless of his activity or nonactivity in the Church. He is devoted to all of us, has provided well for us, and is always available when we need his counsel or help. We have remained a close family, and I believe it will always be that way.

I also believe that family activities, regular family home evenings, and other planned events do more to strengthen family ties than almost anything else. And when family ties are strengthened, so are eternal bonds. Even a child or spouse who is currently openly hostile to the Church may one day reflect on the strength of his or her own family and perhaps use that as the stepping stone to Church membership and activity. Bonding occurs almost imperceptibly as families join together for different occasions.

Maintaining Flexibility

When my husband and I married in the Baptist church, I am sure that he had no idea he would someday be married to an LDS woman, let alone to a professor in the English department at BYU. My realization that I am simply not the person he thought he was getting in the first place has helped me to be patient with him despite his reluctance to jump into full Church activity. Our children have helped, too. The four of them, three active in the Church and one less-active, are treasures to both of us. We share their ups and downs, their accomplishments, and their challenges— as we did when they were still under our roof. Our telephone bills are a little high, and we use email, but our friendships have grown, and we enjoy the times we can be together.

One way we continue to strengthen our ties with children and grandchildren is through family history research. Families throughout the world—nonmembers and Church members alike—are catching the spirit of Elijah through family history work. My husband has in his possession many family artifacts that he holds dear: letters, hand-written and typed histories, and scraps of information that go back several generations. In his heritage are riverboat captains and merchants, farmers and businessmen. He had a well-educated aunt who became a physician against all odds in the early 1900s. His known lineage winds back to the Revolutionary War and ranges from engineers to the owner of a Western trading post. Our children and grandchildren never seem to tire of hearing the stories of these hard-working progenitors.

My heritage has been interesting to trace, too. A stained glass window in the Anglican chapel at Williamsburg bears one of my family member's names. I had ancestors in the Revolutionary War, the Civil War, and the Spanish-American War. One of my family names, Bowles, came from the surmised original Bols, who was said to be a bowl-bearer at the English court of William the Conqueror after the Battle of Hastings in 1066. Francis Bacon was one of my uncles, and William Jenner of smallpox vaccination fame was another.

Seeking and recording our forebears is an activity that has, over time, bound our two families together. In turn, it has also bound the two of us together. It becomes a mutual mystery to find out whose ancestor came over on which ship, or whose progenitor had enough to eat during lean times and whose didn't. It is fun to find the markers in old cemeteries and to photograph them as a visual legacy for our children.

But for me, there is more to our genealogy than simply finding the names and histories. I know that someday we will meet all of these folks; someday we will learn to love these ancestors just as we love the children Heavenly Father entrusted to us. Additionally, I know that I am under strict commandment to have the temple work performed for our deceased ancestors. Joseph Smith "presented baptism for the dead as the only way that men can appear as saviors on Mount Zion. . . . Men, by actively engaging in rites of salvation substitutionally become instrumental in bringing multitudes of their kindred into the kingdom of God" (in *Teachings of the Prophet Joseph Smith*, 191). Vicarious baptisms and other ordinances are being performed for both of our families. I am fortunate that Denny has no objection to my preparing his family names for submission; and friends and family members are helping me do the temple work. Last year I had my father's work done, and then I was proxy for his mother as he was sealed to his parents. It was a sweet moment. Our daughter Valerie did the work for one of our great-aunts. We went to the temple together, and it brought joy to both of us. Though some spouses or extended family members may object to the submission of names for temple work, I believe that objection leads to a teaching moment. Explaining the principles of *choice* and *agency* concerning acceptance of the performed ordinances can inform them and also relieve concerns that they may have.

Expressions of Love

It is important to remember that "nonmembers generally accept the gospel because *they* have been accepted by those who have already embraced it. People are generally converted to people before they are converted to principles. . . . People find it most difficult to be without a friendship circle" (Ernest Eberhard Jr., "How to Help Nonmembers in Your Own Family," *Ensign*, October 1977, 65; emphasis added). Most of our extended family members, on both sides, have their own church-related friendship circles. And I perceive a real responsibility of converted family members to extend a warm and consistent hand of love to these beloved cousins, aunts, and uncles who are active in other churches. Family gatherings, occasional mailings of an interesting ancestor's history, genealogical charts as they are researched and filled in, copies of old photographs, and occasionally a Book of Mormon with a picture and personal testimony are all ways to extend and share both the family and the gospel. The little packages of family lore are always received with a warm thank you, and slowly the family is responding with further information. We are doing the work of the Lord in building close ties that can lead to an understanding and acceptance of the gospel. As one writer said, "Charity—the pure love of Christ—is the universal solvent of hardened attitudes and beliefs" (ibid., 64).

The simple love and pure expression of children toward others in their families can have a great influence for good. A Church member writes of a situation where the influence of righteous, loving seminary students was very effective in leading family members into Church activity:

> In many situations, children probably have a stronger and deeper influence over parents than anyone else. Some years ago I was involved in a pilot program in a seminary in southern Idaho. The participating students learned one or two of the missionary discussions and then presented them to their parents in their homes. Some of these children had inactive or nonmember parents and wanted their parents to be active and sealed in the temple. The intensity of their desires, as they gave the discussions, simply melted the hearts of some of the parents until their interest and desire to become involved in Church service and activity was fully awakened. The president of the stake in which the pilot program was carried out personally reported that it was more effective than any of the programs used previously in activating members and creating a desire in fathers to receive or advance in the priesthood. *Truly a child can lead them, and should be given opportunity to participate in the effort to bring family nonmembers into the Church* (ibid., 65; emphasis added).

In all our family relationships we must remember, always, the need for sincere thought and prayer. The effort has eternal implications, but includes goals that all family members—including the children—can share. Elder Dallin H. Oaks put it this way:

All Latter-day Saints understand that having an eternal family is an eternal goal. Exaltation is a family matter, not possible outside the everlasting covenant of marriage, which makes possible the perpetuation of glorious family relationships. But this does not mean that everything related to mortal families is an eternal goal. There are many short-term objectives associated with families—such as family togetherness or family solidarity or love—that are methods, not the eternal methods we pursue in priority above all others. . . .

The purpose of mortal families is to bring children into the world, to teach them what is right, and to prepare all family members for exaltation in eternal family relationships. The gospel plan contemplates the kind of family government, discipline, solidarity and love that serve those ultimate goals. But even the love of family members is subject to the overriding first commandment, which is love of God (see Matthew 22:37–38) and "if ye love me, keep my commandments" (John 14:15). As Jesus taught, "He that loveth father or mother more than me is not worthy of me: and he that loveth son or daughter more than me is not worthy of me" (Matthew 10:37) ("Weightier Matters," in 1998–99 Speeches, 148).

In Alma 32:23, we learn that the words of truth can be given to us in many ways: "And now, he imparteth his word by angels unto men, yea, not only men but women also. Now this is not all; little children do have words given unto them many times, which confound the wise and the learned."

In our family, at present, are nine grandchildren. As grandparents, we have found time to be close to each of them; they know us, and we know them. Most of our grandchildren are being raised with the truths of the gospel, and it is my prayer that, over time, they will be instrumental in the conversion of their Grandpa Thursby, the "Great Cool One." They remember him in their prayers each day. There are many significant roles grandparents play in the rearing of grandchildren. It is a loving relationship with someone not seen on a daily basis; in a sense it is not unlike the relationship we have with our Heavenly Father. It can help build trust and faith in goodness unseen. It is a role of honor and should be fulfilled with commitment and dedication.

Elder Henry B. Eyring said:

> The child may be absent. The cares of the day may be great. Yet love for the child can be ever present in the parent, coloring and shaping every word, every act, and every choice. I don't know all that is meant by [the following] passage of scripture, but at least part of it is about *the possibility of a change in our hearts*, that our love of the Savior might always be there and growing:
>
> "But charity is the pure love of Christ, and it endureth forever; and whoso is found possessed of it at the last day, it shall be well with him.
>
> "Wherefore, my beloved brethren, pray unto the Father with all the energy of heart, that ye may be filled with this love, which he hath bestowed upon all who are true followers of his Son, Jesus Christ; that ye may become the sons of God; that when he shall appear we shall be like him, for we shall see him as he is; that we may have this hope; that we may be purified even as he is pure. Amen." (Moro. 7:47–48) ("Always," *1998–99 Speeches*, 95–96; emphasis added).

Elder Bruce R. McConkie once said, "Salvation is a family affair" ("Mothers in Israel and Daughters of Zion," *Ensign*, May 1978, 37). The prayers of parents for children, of grandparents for grandchildren, and of children and grandchildren for their parents and grandparents can bind families together in love and bring all to salvation. From our children's and grandchildren's prayers of the heart—and from my own—I know that at some time, on earth or hereafter, most if not all of our family, both the nuclear and extended, will be united in the gospel of Jesus Christ. We will be a Zion family.

chapter seven

Reinventing the Empty Nest

What a blessing it is to serve a mission for Jesus Christ! Two couples of our acquaintance have served missions in Africa, one in Johannesburg and the other in Uganda. Both couples returned glowing with the memories of a great and humble people, a love for the gospel, and a renewed respect and devotion to one another.

The service my husband and I give is of a different nature, but it is wholesome, strengthens the young people of the Church, and lets us grow. I teach and support the youth, and Denny teaches and supports me. I do not know if a mission is in our future; but through the service we now give, my husband and I have been continuing to build our relationship and to help each other, our friends, and our community. Our preparation and qualifications are a bit different from those of couple missionaries, but in our journey we have also grown in love and unity.

In the spring of 1991, I completed the requirements for a master's degree at Utah State University while teaching high school full time. Denny had supported me entirely by handling many of the chores at home as well as providing constant moral support for the large tasks I had undertaken. That same year, Denny qualified for retirement with full benefits. His last few years of employment had left him feeling "overwhelmed, technically inadequate, drained, tired, and probably depressed." I wanted to continue my schooling and earn a Ph.D., we were now empty nesters (our youngest son was twenty-one and in college), and we no longer had any obligations in Soda Springs, Idaho, where we had been living for twelve years. We took the leap and moved back to the Midwest for a three-year academic commitment in Ohio. A bonus was that we would be much closer to my parents in St. Louis.

Moving to Ohio so far from our own children and long-time friends was both exciting and unnerving. I had fasted and prayed before going and had received what I can call an absolute confirmation of the decision. The Lord taught us a sure way to know if our decisions are correct and I have never failed to receive an answer to my queries:

"Behold, you have not understood; you have supposed that I would give it unto you, when you took no thought save it was to ask me. But, behold, I say unto you, that you must study it out in your mind; then you must ask me if it be right, and if it is right I will cause that your bosom shall burn within you; therefore, you shall feel that it is right" (D&C 9:7–8).

Not long after our move, my eighty-two-year-old dad began feeling weak and ill. He was soon diagnosed with advanced lung cancer, and just six weeks after our relocation to Ohio, he was gone. If we hadn't been within a nine-hour drive, we couldn't have spent as much time with him. We were able to go to St. Louis many weekends, spend much-needed time with my mother, and have treasured time with my father. He was clearheaded until he died, but because of a tracheotomy he couldn't speak. He used a pad and pencil and wrote: "So, you will have a Ph.D.?" I said yes, and I told him about the program and my teaching assignments. He smiled and gave me a thumbs-up. My education pleased my dad, whose parents had both been teachers. The last time I visited before he died, he gave me the thumbs-up gesture again. I loved and respected my father. He was a physically active man, and the whole family was thankful his illness didn't stretch out for months or even years. My father's death was very hard for my mother to accept, but we were there to help as we could.

Denny and I loved our life in Ohio. After three-plus decades of rearing children, we were like a newly married couple. We rented a newly built apartment and were able to explore a region of the country where neither of us had lived before. We had been there only a little while when Denny's former employer offered him a position as a consultant for one of their plants about forty miles from our new home in a suburb of Toledo. I was working ten to twelve hours a day, so his work, plus the commute, made our work days even. Our evenings were spent reading, exploring Toledo and the surrounding region, or watching television or videos. We shopped and cooked together and found new friends through the university.

I didn't understand at that time why a woman my age would be a student in graduate school, but I believed I was doing what the Lord wanted me to. Denny had no doubts about my ability to do the work for the Ph.D. I had my doubts. My primary concern, as always, was to please God and Denny; and Den said his primary concern was to support me. So, we both did our utmost to be considerate of one another, and those gentle and consistent efforts worked another metamorphosis in our relationship. After a year or so, we decided to buy a turn-of-the-century red brick home on a tree-lined street just a few blocks from the Maumee River. We enjoyed having many students in for meals and study sessions, and most of our family and many friends managed to visit us there also.

The Lord blessed me with a clear head and an abundance of energy. I liked my professors, though most of them were years younger than I was. The course of study required for a doctorate in American culture studies was enlightening. I learned things about the United States and Canada that ranged from politics to art. I felt very blessed to have that opportunity to study. I had done a rather extensive study of synagogues along the Wasatch Front when I was in my Utah State University graduate program, and of course, I came from a religiously assorted family. My advisors discovered quickly that I was keenly interested in religion and had studied and visited many, many denominations, and they asked me to teach the course on religions in America. I also taught cultural plurality and folklore. When one of my graduate school colleagues learned by way of the grapevine that I was a Mormon, she was totally shocked. She told me she thought that most Latter-day Saint women my age were either dead or still raising young members of huge families. Once, just outside of my office door, she yelled loudly: "Listen up everyone, Jackie Thursby is a [expletive deleted] Mormon!" I was a bit shocked, but we became friends over time.

The three years in Ohio were so extraordinarily full of activity for both Denny and me that they went by almost in a blur. But in the midst of that, we rediscovered that we loved and respected one another very, very much, and that in spite of our differences concerning the gospel, we still had a great deal in common.

The only calling I had in the Church in Ohio was as a visiting teacher. Our bishop was a well-educated man, a Lutheran convert, and he felt that I had enough to do with teaching several classes, taking classes, and writing a dissertation. By the time we left Ohio three years later to return to Idaho for a part-time teaching position at Idaho State University, Den and I had reinvented our relationship and were completely at peace with each other about the

Church. There was no more tension; we had come to a quiet acceptance of each other's views.

Because we were drawing closer and closer in our friendship, and because we liked to spend the weekends together, we had accepted many invitations to various denominations while we were in Ohio. Further, because I was teaching about religions practiced in America, I took students to a variety of denominations for visits and lectures. At one point we enjoyed a tour of historic old churches deep in the city. The tour was called "Holy Toledo," and it was presented with the hope that people in Toledo would begin to use the buildings more. Margaret, our beloved Catholic next-door neighbor, went with us. The six cathedral-like structures were as varied in their outward architecture as they were in their inward tenets. Some of the professors invited Denny and me to the Unitarian Church services in Bowling Green, and we attended there many times. Denny was particularly pleased with this, and I know it helped our relationship. My bishop understood and supported my choices.

Because I quickly learned that I needed something different from my absorbing academic responsibilities, I volunteered a few hours a week at the newly developing Toledo Botanical Gardens. Again Den was supportive and also became involved; we found that we shared a renewed interest in plants and gardening, so we explored local libraries, found books and magazines to inspire and direct us, and redesigned our yard. It was fun to learn about plants at the botanical garden and then try them out in our landscaping. Our yard wasn't stunning, but we enjoyed the process and the time together. We jointly developed a talent; it was relatively inexpensive and satisfying; and it was a good vehicle for meeting interested neighbors.

We also found that we both like to explore "blue highways," the back roads of the United States, and we took several short trips exploring Ohio, Michigan, and Indiana. We are both readers, and we began to recommend books to one another and then talk about them.

Our discovery of shared interests continues today. Though I have never been much of a sports fan, Denny recently invited me to a Utah Jazz basketball game in Salt Lake City. I balked a little, but he said he thought it would be a good experience for me. "Everyone around here ought to go to at least one Jazz game!" he said. The game was close and exciting, and there was so much else going on that I was totally entertained and came out anxious to go again.

It is reinforcing to my faith in our relationship to note that we continue to find so many common interests. President Joseph Fielding Smith wrote the following in answer to a gospel question many years ago:

> The spirits of men were created with different dispositions and likes and talents. Some evidently were mechanically inclined, from them have come our inventors. Some loved music and hence they have become great musicians. We evidently brought to this world some if not all of the inclinations and talents we had there. The fact that one person finds one bent, like mathematics easy and another finds it difficult, may, in my judgment, be traced to the spirit existence. So with other talents and skills. It was these characteristics that enabled our Eternal Father to choose certain individuals for certain work on the earth, such as Adam, Abraham, Moses, and Joseph Smith. The Lord chose Cyrus and named him one hundred years before he was born to perform the work assigned to him on the earth. It is my judgment that thousands of others were chosen for their special fields

because they showed talents and dispositions in the spirit world (*Answers to Gospel Questions*, 5:138–39).

I am an English/history/art type and Denny is a business/ finance/mechanical type. Our continuing to find interests we care about to share and develop together gives me even more curiosity about the probable eternal nature of our friendship. It also reminds me, repeatedly, of my gratitude to Heavenly Father for guiding us toward each other in mortality. I have also learned that there is never a time that the relationship can be allowed to drift; it is well worth keeping our friendship and affection alive. It must be nurtured, much like a tender plant, and as there are core nutrients that assure thriving vegetation, there are core requirements that must be met to assure a thriving, healthy relationship. The relationship must be protected from anything that would threaten its well-being. As Denny commented: "To have a good marriage the couple needs to continually nurture *their* relationship. The requirements of raising children and building careers take a lot of time and energy, but the core of the family lies in the relationship between the husband and the wife. When it starts to deteriorate, the family becomes dysfunctional."

Gary Steggell, in an article titled "Changing Me, Changing My Marriage," gave advice that is particularly appropriate for a marriage where only one spouse is active in the Church: "If you want to improve your marriage, encourage more of what is already working. Pay more attention to the good things your partner is doing, and do more of the things that please your spouse. This approach will refocus your attention and energy in a positive direction, and you may be surprised in the change in your own feelings and in your spouse's attitude and actions" (*Ensign*, January 1997, 59).

Our three years in Ohio were a time for renewal and reinvention of an old, sometimes stale relationship. President Gordon B. Hinckley said, "Marriage is beautiful when beauty is looked for and cultivated" ("What God Hath Joined Together," *Ensign*, May 1991, 74). William Shakespeare once wrote: "Our bodies are our gardens, to the which our wills are gardeners" (Iago, in *Othello*, 1.3.319–21). Like a garden, marriage must be cultivated and attended, which takes time and attention. It must be weeded and trimmed; unwelcome thoughts and selfish behavior must be eradicated. Keeping a positive attitude provides an atmosphere for a growing friendship. I am again reminded of the scripture I heard often in my early years in the Church that helped me to learn that actions really do equal consequences: "There is a law, irrevocably decreed in heaven before the foundations of this world, upon which all blessings are predicated—and when we obtain any blessing from God, it is by obedience to that law upon which it is predicated" (D&C 130:20–21).

In 1995, the First Presidency of the Church issued "The Family: A Proclamation to the World." It begins by reminding us that "marriage between a man and a woman is ordained of God and that the family is central to the Creator's plan for the eternal destiny of His children" (*Ensign*, November 1995, 102). Marriage is a law of God, and "it is by obedience to that law" that blessings in marriages are obtained. Marriage is a partnership, and wise partners help each other to give service along the way.

We are friends with several couples where one of the couple is less active, or not a member at all. One of these couples served a Peace Corps term in Brazil, reaching out in service together to people who needed help. Another couple, also unlikely to serve a Church mission together, take students to various parts of the world to work on ecological projects through the organization called Earth

Watch. I applaud the many couples who are able to go on full-time missions, serve together in the temple, or are called to serve together in callings in the wards or stakes. I believe that in all of these efforts, a most important point is that their joint service serves to strengthen and continue the holy relationship sanctified by marriage. My prayer is that the service shared by other couples will lead to the preparation and ordinances needed to make these relationships eternal.

By setting realistic goals and moving towards them, husbands and wives can fulfill the law of God. There are many kinds of goals: spiritual, familial, financial, emotional, educational, recreational—but the important key to success is to counsel together and set them down in writing. Of eternal goals, Elder Henry Eyring wrote:

"We must have the goal not in our minds but in our hearts. What we want is eternal life in families. We don't just want it if that is what works out, nor do we want something approaching eternal life. We want eternal life, whatever its cost in effort, pain, and sacrifice. Whenever we are tempted to make eternal life our *hope* instead of our determination, we might think of a building I took a look at a few weeks ago" (*To Draw Closer to God,* 161).

Elder Eyring then described a boarding house he once lived in as a single student, where a mother and daughter provided good food and a clean environment. It was okay, but it wasn't a family "like the one from which we came to this earth and the one which is our destiny to form and live in forever" (ibid., 162). To me, in the relationship with a less-active partner, I have been given, along with the goals we hold in common, the sacred responsibility to influence the family through my "effort, pain, sacrifice," and determination to obtain eternal life. The most effective way to fulfill that calling is by prayer, obedience, and a consistent example. I can honor my husband's priesthood, even if he doesn't think about it. It is real, and I share it with him. I can teach our children, who must find their way, as we must find ours.

I must be patient and do my part and trust the Lord to guide Denny, in their time (both the Lord's and Denny's). Then, in addition to the blessings we enjoy in our marriage today, we will qualify for the promised blessings of the new and everlasting covenant.

conclusion

Embracing the Future

Dr. Connie Blakemore gave a talk at BYU in June of 1998 and presented a concept I find helpful. In her address to the student body she said:

> Your beliefs are the lenses through which you see the world. What you believe determines your focus and in turn your actions. You are seeing things as you *believe* they are—not so much as things *really* are, but rather as *you* are. Our challenge is "to finally see as God sees," as Ann Madsen prompts us. (BYU Women's Conference, May 1998). If your beliefs are based on gospel perspectives, your glasses or belief window will allow you to see eternity from a celestial kingdom perspective. On the other hand, if your belief lenses are made from a non-gospel, or worldly prescription, you will see just the opposite and earn your place in eternity in one of the lower kingdoms. So, what you see is what you get—literally. ("Our Spiritual Eyeglasses," in *1997–98 Speeches*, 324).

I believe that my husband and I will be worthy to be eternal companions, sealed by the Spirit of God for all time and eternity. Because I believe that in righteousness, it will be so. For me, perhaps, the experiences I have had and will continue to have are a part of God's tutoring. Elder Neal Maxwell writes: "God seeks to give us tutoring experiences so that if we are submissive, we will have our own first-hand experiences to refer to in the eternities to come. We will have authentic, personal knowledge upon which to rely, not merely accurate abstractions. Since experiential learning is etched deeply into our souls, it is not easily forgotten" (*Not My Will, But Thine*, 98).

After our three-year sojourn in Ohio, Denny and I took a trip West to spend time with the family, and during the visit I was invited to teach as an adjunct professor at Idaho State University in Pocatello. Our two-year experience in Pocatello was unanticipated, but when I look back I can sincerely say, as I have heard many say, "I could see the hand of the Lord in our plans." The time there was significant for both of us. That two years was a time of resting and preparation. Denny met the bishop of our ward there who really loved him. I witnessed in peace and awe Denny's response to the genuine friendship of that dear man.

The bishop and his wife extended a warmth toward us that we had never experienced before. We were made to feel entirely welcome, and the fact that Denny was less active in the Church was never mentioned. Denny and the bishop became dear friends. The bishop had been one of my professors several years before at Idaho State University. He remembered me and did his best to be the most personally caring bishop we had ever met. He golfed often and took Denny with him many, many times. He introduced Denny to people in the neighborhood and even took an active interest in our unmarried son, Will. I've never known a bishop who more thoroughly exemplified the Savior's admonition to "feed the flock of God which is among you, taking the oversight thereof, not by constraint, but willingly; not for filthy lucre, but of a ready mind; neither as being lords over God's heritage, but being ensamples to the flock. And when the chief Shepherd shall appear, ye shall receive a crown of glory that fadeth not away" (1 Peter 5:2–4).

Denny and I both loved our bishop and his wife, and they did their best to help us along the gospel way. She invited me places, and we took exercise walks in the morning. They invited me many times to go on excursions with them to the temple in Idaho Falls.

One of the changes that took place in me while we were in Pocatello was that I had time to study the scriptures more thoroughly. Though I had not stopped reading the scriptures during my graduate programs, I hadn't been what Gayle Strathearn called later, a "scholar of the scriptures":

> "What does it mean to be a scholar of the scriptures?" I sometimes compare studying the scriptures to a rich, multilayered piece of cake, heeding the Lord's counsel to Isaiah to "make the heart of this people fat" (Isaiah 6:10). The layers of a multilayered cake can represent different experiences in our lifetime scripture study. For instance, some layers may represent personal study added on at various times in our life; other layers may represent family scripture study or institute or seminary classes; another layer may represent Gospel Doctrine, priesthood, or Relief Society classes and discussions. Each layer adds to the flavorful richness of our study experience. A scholarly approach to the scriptures adds to that richness ("Studying the Scriptures: A Scholarly Approach," in *Every Good Thing*, 341–42).

I was changing in my approach and understanding of the scriptures, and Denny sensed that. Denny was changing, too. Other than serving on the school board when we lived in Soda Springs and voting regularly, he had never been particularly involved in the community. In Pocatello he began to do volunteer tax work for the elderly, and he became very committed to that responsibility. He also involved himself with a program called Neighborhood Watch. He began to attend Church functions with me with little complaint and few funny remarks.

An attentive bishop can have tremendous influence on a family like ours. Our children, even those who didn't live nearby, got to know our bishop because he would "just happen" to make brief stops at our home when they were visiting. "That way," he said with a twinkle, "I'll know who you are talking about when you say 'Michelle, Chris, Valerie, or Will'!" One Sunday morning he said to me, "Jackie, why aren't you at BYU? You have a Ph.D. and a temple recommend. My wife and I are BYU graduates, and we both have a feeling that you should serve the Lord there."

It seems odd now that teaching at the Church's university had not occurred to me; my only explanation is that somehow, as silly as it may seem, I didn't think Brigham Young University would hire converts. I actually thought you had to have a "Mormon pedigree," as one professor put it, to teach there.

The bishop's wife clearly explained that I had a responsibility to pray and seek the direction the Lord had for me. She also reminded me of my value to him in the work of the kingdom. I went home and began to pray. The feelings I received after praying were comfortable and positive, so I decided to write a query letter. The letter explained our situation as succinctly as I knew how. I enclosed a vitae/resume, mailed the letter, and waited. In a few days, late one afternoon, the phone rang. It was the chairman of the BYU English Department. He said, "Your credentials are interesting to us because we are currently advertising for applicants for two positions in the department, and you have the credentials for both of them. We would like to meet you. Can you come for a lunch visit in Provo next week?

To make a long story short, I was soon offered a full-time position in the English Department to teach myth, legend, and folklore classes, to teach methods for secondary English teachers, and to supervise secondary English teachers during their field experiences. Other assignments included research/writing/publication and community service at the university, in the Church, and in the community at large. Though I wasn't young, we decided to accept the challenge. Underneath everything, I was praying that all of this would work out and that Denny really would like Provo. The home we found needed landscaping, but the inside of the house was clean and freshly decorated. With our shared interest in gardening, that wasn't a problem. The first night we stayed in the house I looked out one of the upstairs windows and was surprised to see the spire of the Provo temple glowing against the background of steep, dark mountains. When I look out that window, it reminds me of Isaiah's words: "And the Lord will create upon every dwelling place of mount Zion, and upon her assemblies, a cloud and smoke by day, and the shining of a flaming fire by night: for upon all the glory shall be a defense. And there shall be a tabernacle for a shadow in the daytime from the heat, and for a place of refuge, and for a covert from storm and from rain" (Isaiah 4:5–6).

It is a joy to live so close to a temple where I can go to learn more of the things of the Spirit. I am likewise grateful for the chance to be at BYU, where I have also learned more of the Lord's methods of teaching.

Though I have been trained in my academic field, there were nuances about teaching and sharing that I felt but really didn't understand. The late Arthur Henry King asked: "What . . . is most precious, if not the knowledge that we are individual persons of infinite worth, having free agency? That is what love starts from. To have love, there must be some sense of the individual; there must be individuals to love and be loved. We can't really love ideas; we can't love abstract notions. We are made to love individuals" (*The Abundance of the Heart*, 23)

Russell T. Osguthorpe, of the Faculty Development Center at

BYU, explained how Brother King's thought could be understood in terms of teaching:

> As parents and teachers we want our children to be so attracted to a topic that they will want to learn more about it. We worry that we may even cause them to hate the topic we are trying to teach them. But when someone dislikes a topic, or an entire discipline, it is because the person does not understand how it fits into truth, how it is necessary to the person and those the person loves, and how it connects the person to God. It is this kind of understanding that we need to seek in our teaching and in our learning. Then we, as either teachers or learners, will be directing our love in ways that not only will help us enjoy the topic we are learning but will result in an increase of love towards others. (*The Education of the Heart: Rediscovering the Spiritual Roots of Learning*, 37).

These words were written for faculty in relation to the students, or to parents in relation to their children, but they also apply to a marriage relationship like ours. Denny has his agency, and I have learned to respect it.

Denny and I seek truth, and we both believe in diligence and obedience to our consciences. President Merrill J. Bateman said, "Two principles govern the acquisition of truth and intelligence. They are *diligence* and *obedience* (compare Alma 12:9). . . . Diligence is one of the laws of heaven that determines the knowledge and intelligence that may be acquired by the earnest truth seeker" ("Secular Learning in a Spiritual Environment," in John W. Welch and Don E. Norton, eds., *Educating Zion*, 239; emphasis in original).

It is of great comfort to me to hear and read these words and know that I am at peace with my husband and his progress.

Denny and I are, of course, growing older, but we are continuing to discover what we love, enjoy, and respect about each other and our family and friends. Margaret, our dear Catholic neighbor and friend who lived next to us in Ohio is still well and studying, traveling, and serving those around her. Earline, though suffering some physical disabilities, is at peace and happy. The last time we spoke on the phone, she said that she and her husband enjoy both of their families and, in fact, had seen her former husband at a family occasion when one of her daughter's children was baptized. Surprisingly, the former husband accepted an invitation, was amiable, and said that he is attending the Church now and then. It was a pleasant surprise for everyone!

Our children and grandchildren are all moving along in positive directions. Their occupations are editor, elementary school teacher, safety environmentalist, and golf professional. Three of the four continue to be active in their wards, and the fourth, like his father, lives a good life and devoutly avoids churches. My mother, the only grandparent in our family now living, is still well and positive. Now ninety-two, she told me that she "can't do much besides pray anymore, but I guess God thinks that's enough reason to leave me living here on earth." I thanked her and told her that was probably what our family needs most. Her stalwart Baptist faith carries her in peace.

This is a positive time, and our lives are becoming richer in the desire to give our time and talents in service to others. Elder Neal Maxwell reminded us that "life is carefully designed to produce for us, if we are willing, a harvest of relevant and portable experience. But there is such a short growing season!" ("Enduring Well," *Ensign,* April 1997, 8).

Denny and I are friends, very good friends. Our marriage bonds are like the covenant a Christian makes with Christ. As Stephen E. Robinson wrote:

As husband and wife become one with each other through the covenant of marriage, so the Savior and the saved become one with each other through the covenant of the gospel. (Cf. 1 Cor. 6:15–17). Just as a bride renounces all competing claims upon her loyalties and normally takes her husband's last name, those who enter this covenant with Christ renounce all competing loyalties, put him first, and take his name upon them. To this union, we bring our righteous desires and our loyalty. He brings his perfection. In the covenant union, what is mine becomes his, and what is his becomes mine. Thus my sins become his for payment, and his righteousness becomes mine for justification. (*Believing Christ*, 24–25).

I have made covenants with belief, understanding, and meaning—both to Christ and to my husband. And because I have not been automatically programmed with wisdom, I have made some mistakes in the relationships. Neither Christ nor Denny have ever abandoned me, but I am sure that there have been times when I have disappointed both of them.

For years I found it interesting that I could be very busy, even consumed, with academic or community responsibilities but have our home and relationship remain at peace. Yet, when I gave time to the Church or Church-related activities, there was a distancing between Denny and me. I thought about this time and again over the years and tried to understand. It is easy to think, as I once did, "Well, that is Satan's way." But, after years of praying and pondering, I finally realized what was happening. The answer was so plain! When I was "doing" Church, I was not sharing. I did not include Denny. I hadn't considered his point of view or asked his opinions. I simply took an independent approach, figuring he wasn't interested in what I was doing and might be irritated if I bothered him with it. Elder Boyd K. Packer, in the 1972 talk he addressed to women with nonmember or less-active husbands, suggested, "Why don't you begin where you are, right at home? And I repeat, if your husband doesn't feel at home going to church, then do everything you can to make him feel at church while he's at home" ("Begin Where You Are—At Home," *Ensign*, February 1972, 71).

I didn't have Elder Packer's article with me in Ohio, but that is where I began to realize the necessary principle of including Denny in *everything* I was doing and, essentially, taking the Church to him. I didn't ask him to move from his comfort zone, but I began to ask him questions relating to my activities at Church. I first asked him for his input on a "Crossing Cultural Boundaries in the Gospel" sacrament meeting talk I was asked to give in my ward. He helped; he came to church to hear the presentation and shared in the discussion and commentary afterward. There was no friction whatsoever. After our move to Idaho, I deliberately asked him to help me with my Church activities if he could. I discussed just as openly what I would be teaching in a gospel lesson as I would if I were preparing for an English or history lecture. Overcoming my fear of offending him, I found that his ideas were valuable and objective, and he was interested in helping.

Elder Jeffrey R. Holland has said:

> The first element of divine love—pure love— taught by these two prophets [Paul and Mormon] is its kindness, its selfless quality, its lack of ego and vanity and consuming self-centeredness. "Charity suffereth long, and is kind, [charity] envieth not, and is not puffed up, seeketh not her own" (Moroni 7:45). I have heard President Hinckley teach publicly and privately what I suppose all leaders have said—that most problems in love and marriage ultimately start with selfishness. In outlining ideal love in which Christ, the most unselfish man who ever lived, is the great

example, it is not surprising that this scriptural commentary starts here ("How Do I Love Thee?" in *1999–2000 Speeches*, 159).

Who, me selfish? I believe that in many ways I was. I didn't think Denny wanted to hear about my Church assignments, I didn't talk about them with him, and therefore I deprived both of us of blessings while illogically feeling sorry for myself.

In my humanness, it took a long time for me to internalize some of these simple points, but honoring these principles will help to build a strong marriage for time and all eternity:

1. Love, honor, and obey the Lord Jesus Christ in everything you do.
2. Treat your spouse as you would enjoy being treated. Respect his or her agency.
3. Love and honor your spouse in every positive attribute and action you can. Notice and validate his or her good qualities.
4. Invite your companion, often, to participate in your activities and support him or her.
5. Be positive. Let your light shine, always.
6. Make your home a place where love can be felt at all times. Care enough to make it a real home.

In his book *Standing for Something*, President Gordon B. Hinckley wrote: "For marriage to be mutually satisfying, there must be recognition on the part of both husband and wife of the solemnity and sanctity of their union and of the God-given design behind it. Husbands and wives, look upon each other as precious companions, and live worthy of that association. Parents, see in your children sons and daughters of the Almighty, Who will hold you accountable for them. Stand together as their guardians, their protectors, their guides, their anchors" (156).

Last fall, Denny accepted an ad hoc calling to build a spook alley in the ward for a Halloween party. He planned, built, supervised, and seemed to enjoy the whole process. I was delighted that he accepted the assignment and was mostly enthusiastic. I like celebrations, although Halloween is not my favorite. The party was a huge success. I supported Denny and the planners and had fun along with everyone else.

President James E. Faust, second counselor in the First Presidency, spoke at the 1996 Sunday morning session of general conference. He began by saying: "Today I speak to those who have heartrending challenges. I speak to those who mourn and have heartaches. I speak to those with physical, mental, or emotional pain" ("Woman, Why Weepest Thou?" *Ensign*, November 1996, 52).

I listened, and he continued:

> All of us benefit from the transcendent blessings of the Atonement and the Resurrection, through which the healing process can work in our lives. The hurt can be replaced by the joy the Savior promised. To the doubting Thomas, Jesus said, "Be not faithless, but believing." Through faith and righteousness all of the inequities, injuries, and pains of this life can be fully compensated for and made right. Blessings denied in this life will be fully recompensed in the eternities. Through complete repentance of our sins we can be forgiven and we can enjoy eternal life. Thus our suffering in this life can be as the refining fire, purifying us for a higher purpose. Heartaches can be healed, and we can come to know a soul-satisfying joy and happiness beyond our dreams and expectations (ibid., 52).

I know that my problems were custom-designed for my capabilities. There are many whose lives are much more difficult. I love my companion and hope, so much, for him to receive the full blessings of knowledge and wisdom provided by obeying the principles of the gospel. As time moves along, we are both increasingly being drawn into service opportunities. Den just built shelves in an elderly neighbor's basement to store inherited treasures, and I have responded to various needs for service as I have seen them. Giving service is Denny's way of living the gospel, and that is clearly what Jesus Christ asked us to do.

Our continued interest in family history has resurfaced, and we are in the process of putting all of our records on the computer. I have attended the temple as often as possible over the years and served as a temple ordinance worker in the Provo temple. I have begun doing more of the temple work for our own families. It is a useful effort for both of us, and I hope it will open the way for our loved ones on the other side of the veil.

Another spring in Provo is nearly upon us. Trees, shrubs, herbs, and bulbs that we have used to dress our yard are awakening. Two of my neighbors noted the three willows in our yard and have nick-named me "Jacqueline of Three Willows." When I told Denny, he reflected that the neighbors were creative but that willows are weed trees as far as he is concerned. He said, "If a good wind comes and splits those trees, it will be 'Jacqueline of Three Oaks.'"

The willows and oaks might be a metaphor for our lives. Willows are large and fast growing and send out water-seeking roots; oaks send down a deep, central taproot. They are slower growing and long lasting. There is little maintenance to an oak, but willows need a lot of trimming and grooming. A stanza of the Primary song, "I Am a Child of God" says, "I am a child of God, and so my needs are great" (*Children's Songbook*, 2). I do need God, my needs *are* great, and the Church has taught me how to have a relationship with him. I need the metaphorical water of life, lots of it. Denny feels more independent and less needy. I believe, though, that he receives of the goodness of God as I do. There is comfort in the scripture in Paul's statement: "If any brother hath a wife that believeth not, and she be pleased to dwell with him, let him not put her away. And the woman which hath an husband that believeth not, and if he be pleased to dwell with her, let her not leave him. For the unbelieving husband is sanctified by the wife, and the unbelieving wife is sanctified by the husband" (1 Corinthians 7:12–14).

Recently, two professors in the English department were kind enough to mark our map of Utah with four day trips. When we are not spending Saturdays working in the yard, we hope to travel through and explore Utah, as we have traveled through and explored life. Just as we will follow the trails marked by the professors, in time, we will both follow the clear gospel path that will take us back to our Heavenly Father together. Sheri Dew reminds us that "a casual commitment to Christ will not carry us through" ("We Are Women of God," *Ensign*, November 1999, 98). That is true. And there will be a time when my husband will know and understand his dependency on God, though that time is not yet.

When we married in 1959, we both committed our lives, "for better and for worse," for life. Later, in 1967, when we were sealed in the Salt Lake Temple, we recommitted to Heavenly Father and each other "for time and all eternity." I love this gentle man. And I know, deep in my heart, that we are on the path to eternal and celestial peace, happiness, and fulfillment. Our destiny is a work in progress, and each day we begin where we are.

appendix

The following articles may be helpful as you "begin where you are" in the work of strengthening ties with loved ones who either struggle in their beliefs or simply do not believe as you do:

Faust, James E. "Woman, Why Weepest Thou," *Ensign,* November 1996, 52–54.

Gardner, Marvin J. "Keeping the Door Open and the Stew Hot: Loving and Helping a Wayward Child." *Ensign,* August 1982, 9–13.

Hancock, "Daughter, Be of Good Comfort." *Ensign,* 79–80.

Packer, Boyd K. "Begin Where You Are—At Home," *Ensign,* February 1972, 69–74.

works cited

1997–98 Speeches. Provo: Brigham Young University, 1998.

1998–99 Speeches. Provo: Brigham Young University, 1999.

1999–2000 Speeches. Provo: Brigham Young University, 2000.

The Arms of His Love: Talks from the 1999 Women's Conference. Salt Lake City: Deseret Book, 2000.

Brothers, Joyce. "Reconnect with Your Family." *Parade Magazine*, 4 November 2001, 4–7.

Children's Songbook of The Church of Jesus Christ of Latter-day Saints. Salt Lake City: The Church of Jesus Christ of Latter-day Saints, 1989.

Conference Report. Salt Lake City: The Church of Jesus Christ of Latter-day Saints. April 1929.

Dollahite, David C., ed. *Strengthening Our Families: An In-Depth Look at the Proclamation on the Family*. Salt Lake City: Deseret Book, 2000.

Ensign. Salt Lake City: The Church of Jesus Christ of Latter-day Saints, 1971–.

Every Good Thing: Talks from the 1997 BYU Women's Conference. Edited by Dawn Hall Anderson, Susette Fletcher Green, and Dlora Hall Dalton. Salt Lake City: Deseret Book, 1997.

Eyring, Henry B. *To Draw Closer to God*. Salt Lake City: Deseret Book, 1997.

Garcia-Prats, Catherine Musco, and Joseph A. Garcia-Prats. *Good Families Don't Just Happen: What We Learned from Raising our 10 Sons and How It Can Work for You*. Holbrook, Mass.: Adams Media Corporation, 1997.

Hinckley, Gordon B. *Standing for Something*. New York: Random House, 1999.

"How to Cope: Father's Inactivity Doesn't Stop Family." *Church News*, 3 January 1981, 51.

Hymns: The Church of Jesus Christ of Latter-day Saints. Salt Lake City: Deseret Book, 1948.

King, Arthur Henry. *The Abundance of the Heart*. Salt Lake City: Bookcraft, 1986.

Lewis, C. S. *The Weight of Glory*. New York: HarperCollins, 2001.

Maxwell, Neal A. *If Thou Endure It Well*. Salt Lake City: Deseret Book, 1996.

———. *The Neal A. Maxwell Quote Book*. Edited by Cory H. Maxwell. Salt Lake City: Bookcraft, 1997.

———. *Not My Will, But Thine: The Christlike Path of Submission to God's Will*. Salt Lake City: Deseret Book, 1988.

Morrison, Alexander B. "Some Myths and Misconceptions about Mental Illness." Address to leaders of Pioneer Welfare Region. Salt Lake City, Utah, 21 April 2001.

Osguthorpe, Russell T. *The Education of the Heart: Rediscovering the Spiritual Roots of Learning*. American Fork, Utah: Covenant Communications, 1996.

Peterson, Wilferd A. *Twenty-Three Essays on the Art of Living*. New York: Simon and Schuster, 1961.

Rasband, Ester. *Confronting the Myth of Self-Esteem*. Salt Lake City: Deseret Book, 1998.

Robinson, Stephen E. *Believing Christ*. Salt Lake City: Deseret Book, 1992.

Shakespeare, William. *Othello*. 1.3.319–21.

Smith, Joseph. *Teachings of the Prophet Joseph Smith*. Selected by Joseph Fielding Smith. Salt Lake City: Deseret Book, 1976.

Smith, Joseph Fielding. *Answers to Gospel Questions, Volume 5*. Salt Lake City: Deseret Book, 1966.

Welch, John W., and Don E. Norton, eds. *Educating Zion*. Provo: BYU Studies, 1996.

index